THE OILY BIBLE

Version 7 - August 2024

For Daniel

Feed your appetite for curiosity and
strive to be your very best.
Be humble, grateful, patient
and forever happy.

Love you to the stars and back.

Pop xx

Thank you for purchasing this book.
I will be forever grateful to you.

This book is a continuum, an incomplete works, which will grow and evolve over time, which is why it is produced digitally (and printed) on-demand.

10% of profits to the mental health charity; MIND (Charity Number: 219830).

Please pay it forward. Pass it on.
Let's try to change a life for the better.

If in a printed, physical format, this book will be made from paper and board sourced from regenerative, managed forests.

Did you know?
Most paper is sourced from the parts of a tree, which is removed during timber preparation.

When you see the Love Paper mark below, it an assurance that paper is sourced from well-managed forests with FSC, PEFC or SFI certification.

www.lovepaper.org

The Oily Bible - Contents

Chapter 1:   Everything Happens For A Reason

Chapter 2:   My Background

Chapter 3:   The Power Of The Universe

Chapter 4:   Quantum Dynamics

Chapter 5:   World Peace 'Hands of Hope'

Chapter 6:   The Life and Legacy of Nikola Tesla

Chapter 7:   The Symphony of Resonance

Chapter 8:   Mind-Over-Matter

Chapter 9:   Focus To Infinity

Chapter 10:   Listening Blindspot

Chapter 11:   Health, Wealth & Purpose

Chapter 12:   Paying It Forward

Finale: Nature's Gift To Humanity

Synopsis

"The Oily Bible" delves into the intricate web of communication and the dynamic flow of ideas and energy in various forms, revealing how these elements shape our everyday experiences.

Blending scientific insights with thoughtful explorations of philosophy, astrology, art, spiritualism, and select esoteric concepts, this book offers a holistic perspective on life.

While it is not a religious text, it boldly challenges conventional notions of our roles, responsibilities, and purpose in the universe.

Bates's journey begins with his personal battle against bipolar disorder, which he describes as a "skillness" that he has transformed into an extraordinary superpower.

He examines the nature of energy - how it is transmitted, absorbed, transformed, and amplified through ancient, harmless techniques that, in many cases, have faded from contemporary knowledge.
Get ready to be both inspired and entertained!

Ian H Bates
www.about.me/ianhbates

About the Author - Ian H Bates

Born in Ipswich, England, 29th September 1964, Bates was diagnosed with bipolar at the age of thirty-eight. This resulted in one failed marriage and the unfolding of some rather bizarre events - some of which are shared in this story, his first published book.

The Oily Bible chronicles his path of enlightened consciousness, whilst maintaining a successful career in media, design, manufacturing and material as well as product development within the world of packaging. He's founded numerous successful businesses and has also had a number of failures along the way. Despite all this, he remains happy, healthy and purpose-driven, helping people and organisations reduce their environmental impacts through better design and communication.

Married with one son, he lives near Maldon in England.

Chapter 1
Everything Happens For A Reason

I awoke from a deep, blissful sleep, jam-packed with fantastical dreams and magical events, which words are inadequate to describe. Had I really just had an encounter with my maker?

Impossible. So I thought...

It's taken me over twenty-five years to untangle a complex web of 100's of years of knowledge and better understand what I might have unearthed. Like all of us, I am still learning. I will never stop. I try to be objective and agnostic so that you can make up your own mind if this is true or utter nonsense.

After all, you only have my word for it.

Enlightenment

Thirty-eight at the time, (now in my sixtieth year) and happily married, I had a good career as a director for an industrial manufacturing group based in Corby, England. I was head of sales, service, marketing and design. All very average and normal you might think? Things were going pretty well until one day everything changed. Like a merry-go-round, I just hopped-off and went in search of a new, more meaningful ride. This time, one with more purpose.

'The awaking', as I call it, happened in the early hours after a day of alpine skiing in Chamonix, France with some friends. For my first time, I smoked an entire marijuana joint the evening before, which was given to me by one of the other guests in the chalet. This joint made me very high so I went off to bed to sleep it off.

Early the following morning, I was awoken suddenly by a powerful force, which I can only describe as a spiritual encounter. As bizarre as it seemed to me at the time, I lay there listening to the single Voice inside my head. This had never happened to me before and I was somewhat surprised and rather bewildered.

This Voice asked me politely to stop everything I was doing and take ownership of my life and fulfil my true purpose. "My true purpose" I asked? *"Let go of everything, live in the moment, be truly happy"*. I was happy, or so I thought, at the time. I was married to a beautiful lady, who had been my teenage sweetheart and we were very much in love. We had three Labrador dogs and lived in a lovely home near Northampton, England. She had a good career in the legal profession and apart from recovering from a terrible horse riding accident, which broke her back some years before, life was pretty rosy. A few years before we were married, my then girlfriend decided to give up our child through having an abortion because she wanted to pursue her legal career and not start a family. This broke my heart and to this day fills me with regret and guilt.

Back to the conversation with The Voice. "I am already perfectly happy thank you", I said. The Voice then said, *"you will need to make some significant sacrifices to fulfil your purpose"*. "And what does that mean?", I asked. *"Your marriage will end soon and you will have a period of emotional struggle, but you will become stronger and ready for your true mission"* The Voice replied. "No, that's not going to happen, why don't you please leave me alone?" I replied. The Voice then said calmly, but firmly said *"Have faith, all will become clear in the fullness of time, I will try to guide you, but only if you agree now"*. I thought about what was happening and instinctively, I replied "Okay, I agree. I trust you".

What happened next made me cry uncontrollably. Weirdly, not with sadness, but with overwhelming joy and happiness. All very strange, I thought. I then asked the next obvious question; "Who are you?". The Voice replied *"I am the all seeing one, RA - The Sun God as I am often referred"*. "Wow, really? So what do you want from me?" I enquired. *"You are one of my sons and I need you to step up on Earth as it is in Heaven"*. "Really? Is this the drugs screwing with my head?". No reply.

The Voice then explained that after my marriage, I would go on a long journey of enlightenment and discovery. This strange conversation only took a few minutes at most. I then climbed out of bed and went for a long, reflective walk through the snowy Alps to clear my head. I walked for miles going over the conversation, trying to make sense of it all. I was excited, sad and somewhat confused.

I met the others for breakfast and they asked if I was okay given that I had been up so early. I replied "yep, never felt better, let's go do some hard core skiing". Clearly, I was still high and I had rather a lot to unpack. Was I going mad? Maybe it was the altitude, mixed with the drugs, alcohol and physical exertion of skiing all day. I was convinced it was the drugs and that things would return to normal pretty soon. The drugs did wear off over the next couple of days, but that was only the start of the craziness.

I returned to work the following week to attend a quarterly board meeting. I asked the receptionist to bring red wine (symbolic or what?) to the board room (called the Gutenberg Room by complete coincidence!) instead of the usual tea and coffee. She asked "what was the celebration all about?". I replied "I have a big surprise for everyone". She looked at me and raised her eyebrows! "Oh, another one of your pranks hey?". I don't remember exactly what I said at the board meeting, but I am guessing it was pretty difficult for everyone around the table to comprehend what I was saying and the owner rightly decided I needed a longer holiday. I do recall talking about Richard the Great and the historical significance of his reign and his links to the Knights Templar and I remember talking expertly about the Holy Grail! I accepted the extended holiday offer without persuasion. How generous, or so I thought. The owner of the company called my wife at work, kindly drove me home and stayed with me until she retuned from her office. What a decent man he was. Early evening there was a knock at the door and three wise men stood there - no only joking - the mental health emergency response team had been dispatched! No white van or restraining suit, contrary to popular belief.

I sat on our large silk Egyptian rug in the middle of the lounge floor sipping tea with these kind and gentle people and they asked me several searching questions. It was a form of interrogation to find out how crazy I might actually be. I tried to answer the questions seriously, but my mood was so elevated and my thought processes somewhat 'connected' that maybe what they heard probably sounded like I had a screw loose. They became quite annoyed with me and at one point said "you have a choice, we will either commit you to our facility or you can come of your own free will. It's your choice". That threat really annoyed me. "Am I a danger to anyone including myself and do I actually have a choice?" I asked. They said "your wife has asked that you comply with us or you will be involuntarily committed". I thought about it for a few minutes and decided to accept their offer, thinking maybe that this was all part of the masterplan of me just accepting the natural order and flow of life. I also thought that the experience would be interesting if nothing else and that I could write about it later! So it was agreed, I was checked-in to St. Andrews Mental Hospital in Northampton, one of the best psychiatric facilities in the UK, under the care of a leading consultant called Mr. Ian Wood. What a wonderful man he turned out to be and we hit it off rather well.

I then spent the next three weeks at St. Andrews being treated for bipolar disorder, also known as manic depression. I attended all the cognitive behaviour therapy sessions, meditation, art and craft groups and played golf and tennis most days. What an amazing facility at a cost back then of over £250 per day. I had a great time and never felt better. I actually felt a rather guilty because some of the people there were very unwell and several people were suicidal. I met some wonderful characters and they became good friends. Everyday the sun shone and I felt on top of the world. Even my brother, who visited me was envious. He even wanted to stay, which was never going to happen! Some friends visited, some didn't including my wife - she found it all too difficult to deal with and probably embarrassing too. This was clearly not good for her reputation. I started painting again and Mr Wood jokingly called me 'Picasso' - probably part of his positivity pep-plan, along with the little pink tablets to bring me gently back to terra firma. The medication definitely worked, but it took a while to manage the dosage correctly so that I was not completely comatose. I am told that one of my acrylic paintings is still hanging on the wall of the clinic. I will go and visit one of these days.

One of the funny things that happened while I was at St. Andrews was my visit to the local Jaguar dealer. The X-Type had just been launched and I asked if I could test drive it. The salesman was only too happy to oblige. We drove for about 30 minutes and I asked toward the end of the test drive, "can you please drop me off at St Andrews Hospital"? He looked at me enquiringly and agreed. Poor chap - another time-waster, he probably thought. I went for the Audi A4 - a much better car it turned out!

Did The Voice and, later, other communications stop? Oh no! It turned into an ensemble of ever-complex communications, which I can only describe to you as super intelligence operating at the speed-of-light. I will explain in plain English later and try to connect the dots between science, philosophy and spirituality. It's a fascinating arc - joining light, energy, life-forming processes and the absorption and transfer of energy at different wavelengths from one particle to another in an infinite continuum beyond time and space. Yep, that all sounds rather complicated, but I will try to explain with proven scientific facts how this might all work. I will help connect the dots and the outcome might surprise you.

As you might expect, I was officially labeled 'bonkers' for which I am grateful. I really am. I felt I had a gift (as we all do incidentally) and although this included being labelled 'mentally ill' at least I was in good hands. I just want to take this opportunity to thank all my wonderful family and loyal friends for standing by me and providing the necessary light relief and distraction to prevent me from becoming too obsessed and depressed at dealing with my new baggage. It's taken me over 25 years to commit to explaining what actually happened. I really hope it will help other people and their family and friends who find themselves in a similar situation.

I write this book with love, passion and wonderment for what this could mean for humanity in a positive context and all that supports life on Earth - humans, fungi, trees, plants, animals, minerals, nutrients and so on.

We are ALL connected, whether we like it or not.

Chapter 2
My Background

I was born in England in 1964. I majored in chemistry, biology and mathematics at 'A' level and went on to study a degree in marketing at Nene College, Northampton - now a university. I should have been an artist, architect or perhaps even a carpenter, but my Dad wanted me to pursue a more academic career. I've no doubt, on reflection, he was right. I love making and creating physical things, which I can then gift to friends and family.

My Dad worked in the pharmaceutical and beverages sectors heading-up purchasing and supply and my Mum followed her own career as a personal assistant to numerous company directors, whilst tending to her flock. My Dad's father was a Methodist Minister and my Mum's father was senior manager working for one of the UK's leading retail banks. Apparently, I very much look like and take after my Mum's father. He was a risk-taker, very confident and loved speeding his Norton motorcycle up and down the very steep Porlock Hill in Somerset, England. Over the years we have lived in Suffolk, Gloucestershire, London, Lancashire, Essex and Hampshire where my parents retired and died a few years ago. We were a bit like gypsies you might say!

Mum and I were very close and I don't think we ever had a crossed word. I loved her dearly and so miss her.

She still visits me spiritually, quite regularly on request. I miss my Dad equally, but our relationship was complex, mostly in a good way. Typical Father, pushing his little boy to be his very best. He was pretty strict, a stickler for detail and frugal with everything. I remember him always asking us to turn off the lights and he would often be found cutting-up cereal cartons into to-do lists and would do anything to save money and waste. He was also hilarious, the life and soul of a party. Both my parents had a wicked sense of humour and joke-telling was always on the menu. Some evenings were spent just telling funny stories and jokes. Happy memories. Both of them taught me a wide spectrum of personal skills and ingrained important life values for which I am very grateful. They were decent, humble, thoughtful, generous and kind people.

My brother and I are very close and speak regularly (usually in daft voices, impersonating famous people like Mrs. Doubtfire - my brother's favourite) and sometimes we holiday together as families. He is so funny, a true entrepreneur and one of the best negotiators I have ever seen in action. He is also very popular, kind and generous - just like our parents.

I have an older sister too, who I respect for her immense intellect and Mother Teresa-like kindness. She's always helping people and working hard. She is also very well read and often encourages me to read more with great book recommendations. She teaches mindfulness and guides young people through her counselling at one of the top private schools in the country. She's one of my go-to people to help me untangle mental knots because I can always count on her for being completely frank with me. She tells me things I sometimes don't want to hear. For example, the cover of this book, was her choice. Created by ChatGPT. It was the only option that she thought projected a positive, up-lifting message. The other options were a bit dark, serious and perhaps a little frightening for most people!

I had a blissful upbringing, apart from witnessing my Dad 'fly off the handle' on the odd occasion when he did not get his way. He was never violent. When I was about eighteen and still living at home, he told me to leave because I swore at him. He let me return a day later, once I apologised and promise never to be rude and disrespectful to him again. I took refuge with a friend who lived just across the road. I was a little bit frightened of him at times as were some of my friends. If he didn't like you, he made it abundantly clear. After my first manic episode, I told him honestly to his face what I thought about his fiery and sometimes blunt behaviour. I really laid into him and off-loaded years of pent-up frustration of how I thought his parenting skills had room for improvement. I was so brutal, I thought he was going to have a heart attack. It was truly awful. I really felt terrible afterwards, but in all honesty he actually deserve it and this episode helped cement our relationship. The following day he started treating me like an adult. It is hard to be specific, but I always felt a tinge of jealously from him. Perfectly natural, because my relationship with my Mum was so special with unconditional love. She just wanted me to be happy and healthy and was always their to encourage and never judge. My father, on the other hand, was not so easy win his approval. He could be highly critical and lacked the ability to show empathy and just say "well done, I'm proud of you". Not once did he ever say he loved me. Not once. I find that rather sad and was properly a reflection of his own upbringing. I know loved me dearly and was very proud of my achievements because my Mum would often tell me quietly when he was not in earshot. Quite early in my career, I pulled up on to the drive of our family home and was greeted by my Dad. I proudly told that this was my new company car - a smart new British Racing Green 323 BMW with cream leather seats. He said something like "really, I had to work all my life to earn a company car". He was clearly not happy for me and green with jealousy. What a shame.

"O beware, my lord, of jealousy; It is the green-eyed monster which doth mock the meat it feeds on."
Act 3, Scene 2, Othello by William Shakespeare.

As you might have gathered by now, I was a 'mummies boy' as my wife often reminds me!

Oh how I miss them both.

Growing up, sport was my thing - running, volleyball, basketball, football, cricket, skiing, roller-blading, cycling being my favourites. One sports day at the age of ten, competing in a 100 meters track race in record time, I had my first asthma attack. This frightened my teachers so much that they tried to stop me from competitive running. I ignored them. Turns out, like many of us, I was just allergic to pollen and house dust. I've always pushed myself hard and sometimes been over-competitive and I guess it is this drive and ambition that pushed my mental capacity to its limits without taking appropriate rest and relaxation.

Married with one son, Daniel, I have a pretty normal life - whatever that means. My wife is in communications and I part own a company and work for a not-for-profit working within the paper and paper packaging sectors. My son has a degree in Spanish. He's passionate about watersports - sub-aqua diving, surfing and anything to do with enjoying and preserving nature. He is actually my step-son and sadly his father died from cancer during the pandemic, but fortunately he was able to be at his bedside when he passed and was also able to attend his funeral, which took place in Australia. It was recorded live via YouTube so we where able to watch and listen to him make the most wonderful eulogy. This was one of the proudest moments of my life - to witness your offspring hold themselves so steadily at such a difficult moment. Only a truly developed sole can do that. Oh, how we cried. His Father and I became good friends and despite the separation, we all united in the most wonderful way. Thank goodness we did. A tribute to my wife and my son's step-mum. The wider family have benefited enormously and this has enabled Daniel to adjust to the tragic loss of his Father at such a young age.

My wife and I met when we were in our early twenties whilst we were both working in London. We lived locally to each other in Essex, after my Dad's work required another relocation. We met at a political event and she arrived late due to a delayed train, but our group went on afterwards for drinks at a local pub. We started chatting and became great friends. I already had a girlfriend, but she lived in another county over 200 miles away and after discovering that she was sharing me with another chap, I explained to her how important monogamy was to me and that our relationship was abruptly over. I forgave her a few years later and we married in Florence, Italy. Sadly this marriage was short due to her cheating on me yet again. It's true; leopards never change their spots.

My 'new' wife and I have been married for over seventeen years. She has a heart of gold, broad shoulders (metaphorically speaking) and is a true angel. I've never met a kinder, more capable, humble and kind person. I frequently drive her nuts and she worries like all good wives do, but she has the capacity to somehow keep the ship steady, as we navigate life's choppy waters.

Has bipolar held me back during my career? Absolutely not! It has without doubt presented some significant challenges along the way for family, friends and colleagues, but provided they know how to support you when you are experiencing a high or low period, in my case, it has been manageable due to my wife's determination and support. This is provided that I take the Sodium Valproate medication daily, drink plenty of water, take regular exercise and have a balanced diet. Oh yes, and make sure I have plenty of R&R. Avoiding bungee and parachute jumps and the production of too much adrenalin is also helpful! When in a manic phase, I tend to become very animated, think and speak quickly and behave out of character. I also become very generous, wanting to gift people with books or other items I think they might appreciate. It's funny, but I have this strong desire to declutter my life of physical objects.

During an interview for a senior directorship a few years ago, the chairman asked me how I coped with stress at work and I openly told him about my condition. He seemed genuinely interested and asked me several questions as to how I managed day to day. He was also open with me about a private matter. I left the interview, jumped in my car to head home and rang my wife. I told her how it went - rather well I thought. "He was great, I liked him and I told him about my bipolar" I said. She was not happy with me, being quite so open and predicted, that I would not be offered the job and that perhaps I should be more cautious and less open in the future. I disagreed with her and said "if they don't like the truth, then I'm not right for them and vice versa". I was offered the job that day. Part of the reason was my openness and honesty. This is rare in corporate life - openness and honesty. Clearly this man and the other directors are good people who could see beyond the challenges of working with someone with a mental disorder. I am very grateful for this leap of faith and loved my time working with these people and for the company, which took me to some amazing places like Delhi, Hong Kong and other parts of the world.

More recently, before being offered an employment contract with my current employer, I suggest to my boss (incidentally, he hates me calling him 'the boss') I insisted that he read a draft of this book. He kindly agreed. The following week he said "I've read your book. Wow, it brought be to tears on occasions and really made me think". I asked "tears of joy or pain?". He replied "both". My contract was issued the following week and I have just been invited to join the board of directors. Just proves that honesty and openness does pay off and if you're punished for any reason, then it's time to move on. You'll probably achieve more elsewhere.

I often remind people that several smart individuals have been diagnosed with bipolar on the including Winston Churchill, Mel Gibson, Mariah Carey, Carrie Fisher,

Jimi Hendrix, Earnest Hemingway, Spike Milligan and Stephen Fry. It never held them back - on the contrary.

For me, honesty and integrity trump everything. You are what you are and hiding the truth will only cause problems later.

Be yourself, be authentic and people will respect you for that.

Chapter 3
The Power Of The Universe

The Oily Bible is not a book about religion. The last thing I want to do is offend people with firm beliefs from a particular culture. I've no doubt, they all have their merits and I respect them equally, but don't fully understand each religion enough to provide an experts view. Some religions do seem to me to be rather myopic, in some cases repressive and lack what I believe to be the importance of an open mind; exploring all the possibilities without judgement.

This book explores communication and the transition or ideas and energy in all forms and how this is conveyed through everyday life across the universe. I try to compare this to the Natural World where light and other forms of electromagnetic energy are converted by all organisms into bio matter, which is then consumed or transferred over time into organic and inorganic forms. Our collective unhealthy relationship and addiction to fossil fuels is discussed at some length and how we might resolve the existential crisis of global warming.

Some of the ideas I present are science-based with a healthy consideration for history, philosophy, and spirituality. I have always been fascinated by people, nature, symbols, design, colour and how things are created, produced, decompose, reassemble and regenerate. I am also interested in how we can manifest ideas from thoughts, vibrations or resonance, mind-over-matter and individual and collective actions to change behaviour of future outcomes.

Most people that know me would probably describe me as slightly odd, sometimes obsessive and driven to preserve our planet and all of its natural beauty. That is all true, but I would also argue that I am completely sane (most of the time), rational, pragmatic and concerned for our planet, which is slowly, but surely being polluted and destroyed via the developed nations' desire to consume and extract at an alarming rate. Just in the UK alone, we consumer six times more energy compared to someone living in India. If everyone on the planet lived like an average westerner, we would need at least six planets. Crazy and avoidable, if we just put our minds to it. In 1760 the Industrial revolution started in England and our unhealthy dependency for coal and other fossil fuels continued to grow exponentially as we've move from the agricultural age to be one powered by industrialisation and digitisation. Here we are, 264 years later, witnessing the impacts of carbon-based gas emissions, through global warming and the impacts this is having on climate change. Mother Nature is unable to cope with our voracious appetite for our economic growth, 'hoarding and upgrading of things' and as developing nations become more 'westernised', this imbalance with nature, will likely become more problematic.

My professional work has been focussed on helping organisations reduce their carbon footprint through better design, material choices and removing unnecessary materials and processes, which are both energy and carbon intensive. I try to use the design principals of 'Cradle to Cradle' originally conceived by Michael Braungart and William McDonough. For me, design and manufacture have always been about collaborating for the greater good, irrespective of the consequences and issues associated with intellectual property and competitiveness. To my mind, Mother Nature is the true master and until we embrace that reality, we jeopardise our ability to collectively thrive. Politics, religion and economics aside, we currently only have one planet, which we share and are temporarily custodians maintaining it in good order for future generations. Moving to another planet, such as Mars, in my view is not practical and will only cause unintended, possibly disastrous consequences. We will not stop the Mars Mission, but I hope we learn lessons along the journey to rethink how we can all live in harmony, reprioritising Mother Nature as the driving-force of the design process and Source of Life.

Energy cannot disappear, it can only transition from one state to another. A good example of this is when you shine a beam of light through a prism and the light refracts into multiple colours of the rainbow all with a different wavelength. These colour wavelengths are detected by the irises in our eyes and our brain decodes each wavelength into a colour palette of information. Quite incredible when you think about it.

In the case of sound, a particular frequency creates movement of the air particles and hair follicles in our ear drums translate each sound wave, which our brain can interpret. When light or sound hits a 'solid object', the energy will partly deflect and some is absorbed in the form of thermal or kinetic energy. All these principals are explained in the science of <u>thermodynamics</u>, which I am not going to go into here, as this is **not** a book about science, moreover the importance of science to explain why our relationship with energy is essential for life.

It is curiosity that has brought me to this point, learning about the relevance and connectedness of everything. Everything, down to the last quark, lepton, boson, gluon, photon, Higgs boson, planke and electron connected in a magical way. Time is irrelevant in a quantum universe and unlike physical objects and liquid, we perhaps all have the ability to travel through time and space if we just put our minds to it. To achieve this, we need to recalibrate to the natural rhythm of nature and disconnect from the buzz of our hectic lives.

If you've ever meditated for any good length of time, you'll appreciate what might be possible.

We are all familiar with the five common human senses - sight, sound, smell, touch and taste. Imagine how they might have been discovered when we were first started humanity. Are there more senses, which we have not yet discovered or agreed upon a suitable label to describe them? I think so. We believe that we know what the sixth sense means, but do we really? Are we agreed on a common language for this rather subjective sense, which is harder to describe for most people. I would argue that it is the sixth and other senses that still to be fully explored and understood. I recently asked a close friend, and a highly developed soul, how many senses did he think he possessed. His answer was "seven". He explained the sixth and seventh senses to me and they made complete sense. He described them as a combination of instinct and emotional intelligence. Both terms are well known, but not scientifically proven or fully analysed and understood.

I think of senses like dimensions. In the first dimension we have a starting point or dot. In the second dimension we have two dots perhaps connected by a line. In the third dimension we have three dots to create a triangular shape. Now imagine a plumb line. The top of the line is the first dimension, the second the weight, connected by a cord and the third dimension is the plumb line, like a pendulum swinging from side to side. The forth dimension is where rotation moves the weight into a circular movement. Now imagine the weight moving in the figure of eight to create a continuous infinity loop. Energy can move 360° in all dimensions at any point in time because it is non-linear and does not require a cord to connect.

When you look at the randomness of the design of a flower, for example, the shapes are typically non-linear and chaotically organic. That's partly what makes them so beautiful and helps us to appreciate their magnificent structures. However, they are very cleverly designed to maximise strength, optimise resources and flexible enough to reach for light, water and nutrients whilst avoiding damage from external forces. As a creative, I find this all fascinating. Knowing that in a forest, underneath the trees and roots, there exists a massive network of mycelium transferring nutrients and information from one tree, plant and fungi to another. They also use insects and other life-forms (including humans) to transfer their energy.

How does it all work?

Well, we are not entirely sure yet, but as science evolves, we will undoubtedly discover the true power of these vital connections. I recommend reading <u>Entangled Life</u> by Merlin Sheldrake to find out more about this mysterious and magical world. <u>Fantastic Fungi</u> is a documentary film on Netflix, which argues that humans might have evolved from fungi, which is not proven, but does present some interesting questions about our origins.

Western societies' addiction to consumerism, time and money is well known and mostly understood. In my personal view, it has become a toxic cocktail, which simply can't be sustained. The clock rules our lives and we appear to be on a merry-go-round, which is spinning faster and faster and often out of control.

It's not clear who actually invented the sundial, but the credit seems to sit with the Egyptians in 1500 BC and they used it to measure the position of the sun during the day. However, it was the Sumerians in Mesopotamia who developed the first calendar in the Bronze Age 2510 BC, which divided a year into 12 lunar months helped by star and planet alignments. The Egyptians adapted this and added a star named Sirius to help keep track of time, keep order and manage events. Hourglasses and water clocks were also developed to keep track of time. The idea for the first mechanical clock is credited to Galileo. However, the first pendulum clock was invented by Christian Huygens in the mid 1600's. Our obsession with time has, like our appetite for consumerism, grown exponentially ever since. And nature's own seasonal clock? Well, that has always been timeless, frequently forgotten and increasingly ignored at our peril it turns out.

We seem to be obsessed with measuring in units of time. Success, failure and even happiness are measured using units of time. When did you last take the day off unplanned and just did nothing, but walk, breath and enjoy the countryside or time getting to know yourself better? Precious time away from the hustle and bustle. For some, this will be a frightening prospect because to keep busy will stop us thinking about what might be missing. Being busy keeps us distracted and unconscious, marching to the beat of the 'industrial economic drum'. We are literally hypnotised and we don't even know it…yet. Some might argue that this is intentional. All part of the plan to keep our hands and minds busy, whilst the real work of evolution can continue without the vast majority of people interfering. Perhaps a conspiracy theory, but I have increasingly wondered if there is some truth in this. Perhaps when you've finished reading this book, you'll have your own views. I'll be pleased to hear from you.

I try to look at my life like this; what would I do if I had a few days to live and was not allowed to tell anyone I was terminally ill, and did not have the opportunity to say "goodbye" to my family and friends? How would I behave and what would I do? What would my relationship with time and my remaining physical life be like and how would I spend those final moments? Interesting questions, which I often ponder.

When you look at the happiest people, they have one thing in common; they truly appreciate what they have and don't allow what they don't have to bother them. In short, they are grateful and content. They are comfortable in their own skin and don't need their ego polishing for their own benefit. Funnily enough, I believe that this is partly the secret to a happy and healthy life. Easy to say, not so easy to do unless you are truly conscious.

When I did finally 'hit the wall' and was diagnosed with bipolar, I learned a very important lesson. That lesson, was to be more accepting of others and try to go with the natural flow of life. Any creation should be to help improve life and I use my own gifts to help others be their best and hopefully be happier. Part of the purpose of publishing this book. Simple, but like all simple things, often over-looked and under appreciated. A great book to read about just going with the the natural flow of life and the benefits can bring is <u>The Surrender Experiment by Michael Singer</u>.

When I am in a manic phase, it lasts two - three weeks. It starts with interrupted sleep and higher energy levels than normal. I typically wake up in the early hours. In recent years, I have used these quiet periods to meditate. It starts with voices in my head, which I try to record, when possible, what is being communicated. I do this by candlelight so as to try not to disturb everyone. I also try to walk in the dark to understand what it's like not to be able to see. I find this optimises my other senses and makes me more aware of my body movement and pent-up energy. Obviously this can be rather dangerous so if you do try it, please be careful. Also be careful with candles as they can easily be left burning and be knocked over when your are in a meditative state. I recommend only using church-size candles on a solid, non-flammable stand, which are far safer. I've nearly burned the house down on a couple of occasions!

Of course, it's not easy to observe and interpret everything. After all, we are human and we have to earn a living, eat, rest and recuperate. We only have so much mental and physical capacity. However, when I completely unshackle my mind, allow chaos to organise itself, the universe does eventually help you go with the natural flow. Like magic, everything synchronises in perfect harmony. The voices seem like normal conversations and are a guide to whatever you might need to know beyond your normal day to day life. Is this communicating with the spirit world? Probably. I do know that if I am trying to solve a particular challenge and I ask for help, in the right way, this help will present itself in the most timely and wonderful way. Our utilised brain capacity is under 20%, which begs the question "what's the rest actually doing?". The meditation normally lasts less than a couple of hours and after a few days of doing this, the skin on my forehead is very dry as if it has been burned by energy in a circular shape. I believe that this is known as the 6th chakra or Third Eye and gateway to inner consciousness, which is well documented. If you would like to learn more about this subject and the power of spiritual healing and all related subjects, I recommend reading anything by Deepak Chopra.

Back to The Voices. If this has never happened to you, it is rather like being guided by a benevolent force and it is extraordinary. I keep asking "so what's possible, if I put my mind to it?" The answer that comes back? *"Anything, you just have to put your mind to it and truly commit yourself"*. Of course, not all forces are benevolent so you do need to be careful. I had a frightening experience when I was about fifteen years old with a Ouija board, which I did not take seriously. After that, I realised that there are powerful forces, which should be respected and better understood. When my voices first started, I was completely overwhelmed. In retrospect, I wish I had found guidance, but I didn't really know where to go. What would I do now? Perhaps seek the advice of a spiritual guide with a good reputation? I'm not going to recommend anyone here because you have your own journey to follow and it's not for me to introduce you to a guide.

As outlined earlier, I capture The Voices in my head by writing and sketching quickly. This then helps me to translate the complex communications later when I'm out of a meditative state. Some of the messages are similar to translating ancient symbols. Very confusing at times. It's as though different languages are being conveyed or the use of words I think I hear are not always correct. A burning candle in a quiet room when it's quiet and dark with as few distractions as possible is best for me, but as I become more practiced, I can zone-in and out without appearing to behave weirdly in the company of people. I do sometimes speak outwardly to a voice and have to stop myself if anyone is watching or listening. The last thing I want is to end up being sectioned and locked-up!

I have tried to write this book several times over the years, but kept stopping to ask myself "why do this and subject myself to the pain and embarrassment of it all?". The answer is always "*Just do it and you'll be glad when it's finished*". I really do hope this helps anyone who has voices in their head and is trying to fathom out if they're going crazy or not. I think it is all pretty normal and is more common than we perhaps realise. Most people have a conversation with themselves - usually in their head, but do not necessarily admit to it. I talk to myself all the time, particularly when I'm out and about walking with my dog. It does get embarrassing at times when you are overheard by a passer by, but then most people now wear ear-pods or headphones so it is quite normal to hear someone talking or singing to themselves!

This might all seem completely normal to you as you might have had similar experiences, but have not felt comfortable sharing your enlightenment! That's what it is, enlightenment. A growing of your consciousness, which is perfect healthy. We were born with these powers, some of us just forgot how to use them growing-up, being moulded into how to behave and think.

Pressures of time and life just get in the way. "Tic Toc" as I often say to people trying to rush me along whilst I am enjoying the natural pace of life. There are those reading this chapter who are already enlightened and do not want to share their secrets. I understand and respect that position. We are all in a varied state of consciousness, just some are more awakened than others, but I do believe there is a change taking place partly thanks to the speed at which people can now communicate. You only have to read ex Google X Innovation head, Mo Gawdat's books '<u>Scary Smart and That Little Voice in Your Head</u>' to understand the power of artificial and super intelligence and the part we might play as we become more connected and hopefully enlightened. AI could be a total disaster for humankind, but it could also be a triumph if managed carefully and positively and not abused by people with unhealthy intentions.

My sister gifted me the short book '<u>The Secret</u>' by Rhonda Byrne for my 42nd birthday and I did not get around to reading it until several years later. It sat on the bookshelf just gathering dust. The author explains the power of attraction and what we think about, we bring about and how outcomes are manifested once we commit ourselves. I recommend reading it, if you have not done so already. It's also available as a movie. If someone now gives me a book or recommends one to me for whatever reason, I now read or listen to it as quickly as possible.

I take the view that people generally want to help you and they only make a recommendation for positive reasons. There can be exceptions of course. One of my other favourite books is 'Human Design' by <u>Chetan Parkyn</u>. I read this in my 40's and I knew then that I had so much to learn, which I would probably never truly understand. I'm starting to appreciate only now.

I often reflect what the planet would be like if you could bring together the best minds, past and present, from the arts, sciences, astrology, spirituality and philosophy. If you could distil all this wisdom and knowledge. Just imagine what could be possible? So what's the short-circuit to this wisdom? Neither of us have the time to read and absorb all this information and experience. Reading and listening to developed people certainly helps.

I think it will come from a combination of applying artificial intelligence to better effect, great collaborations and partnerships and an awakening of more people. We will hit bumps in the road relating to trust, but when we go with the flow and reduce protective behaviour, the magic can happen if we want it to. Profit and greed will be barriers because when you remove the veil of what is possible, everything becomes eminently possible. I have worked on some very challenging projects and, at the outset, we knew there would be many risks and frustration, but piece-by-piece obstacles were overcome and eventually a solution was found. It's all about belief, conviction, having hope and never giving-up.

I see a planet powered by nature for nature and every living inhabitant. A perfect symbiotic relationship where energy, and therefore matter, can flow naturally within the rules and construct of Gaia. In Greek mythology, Gaia is the Goddess of Earth and daughter of Chaos. Chaos was the mother of Uranus (Heaven). At this point, you might think that I'm going to go all religious, philosophical or scientific on you. I am not going to do that. Why, because the majority of readers will switch off. I will say this, every single one of us is unable to fully understand and appreciate the power of the universe unless you connect all the dots simultaneously. So how do you do that with one brain and in one life time? Impossible? Maybe not with some help from AI and quantum processing. We will talk more about the power of AI and quantum, super intelligence later.

For now, some of the answers are surprisingly simple. STOP. Slow down. Observe carefully. Be guided by your own wisdom and instinct. This does take patience and practice because there are so many teachers to learn from and signposts to follow, but like any journey, it is each step-by-step that counts, the direction of travel, not the end objective that are most important. Maybe reflect on that for while before continuing....

Rather like preparing a delicious meal, you start with an idea of what you want to cook, select a recipe, who you are going to invite, select the carefully chosen ingredients and then prepare the meal. There are many other part steps within each action, but you get the gist. Start with a good plan and be prepared to adjust as you go.

To reach true inspiration and therefore potential contentment and happiness, you need to surrender to your teachers and guides. This takes considerable faith and trust and with that you will need to select your teachers and guides carefully because there are good ones and not so good ones. The good guides will only help you if your idea or mission is with good intentions and in harmony with your immediate surroundings and in-sync with Gaia. By good intentions, I mean gratitude and love.

If we accept that we are part of a greater being, we will only be able to start our own journey when we love and appreciate ourselves, everyone around us and everything along our path. Many people do not love or appreciate themselves and never move off first base. I believe some people only discover this reality just before they die. We come into this world with nothing (physical), we leave with nothing (physical). It's up to us if we want to depart happy having led a fulfilled life. Sure, there are going to be challenges, disappointments and sadness along the way, but if you think of these experiences as lessons and not just bad luck, then your perspective and attitude will change. Two of the happiest and sadist days of my life were the funerals of my parents. I was sad to lose them, but they left the most wonderful memories and apart from teaching me how to love and be loved, whilst being a decent human being, they gave me the gift of life for which, I will be eternally grateful.

Creating the right environment to spend time to relax and meditate is vital. You can't be creative or reflective sat around a table on a hard chair. You need to create a space, which enables energy and thoughts to flow. For me, the lighting is also important. Too bright does not work. Candlelight and quietness work for me. You also need to be aware and awake and not falling asleep, so adopting the right position is important. There are many good books on how to meditate and practice mindfulness and gain some level of control over an active, healthy mind. Here's a list from Waterstones. Famous inventors like Nikola Tesla and the founder of Apple, Steve Jobs, are well known for being active meditators.

The connections are certainly complex and difficult to draw logical conclusions. The point I am making is that as humans we are far more capable than perhaps we realise. Try creating space for deep thought and reflection, it does not happen in an instant. It takes practice, patience and guidance along the way to capture the full power of our minds individually and collectively.

I know from being a creative person that no one idea was ever really unique, but a combination of ideas brought together in a new structure or recipe. A great idea is sometimes an old idea using a new process, which makes it work better. The development of new technology is making these discoveries easier and faster to evolve at pace and scale. For example, the rapid invention of Covid vaccines in 2020, which were developed and produced at scale in a matter of months thanks to unprecedented collaboration, political will, automation, AI, computing power and modern distribution systems. Imagine this level of capability to resolve the energy crisis and in doing so reduce the impacts of global warming. It is possible, if we put our minds to it and overcome the political, legal and commercial barriers. Will we do it? Well, the survival of our planet is at stake and I have no doubt only so much suffering and displacement will take place before we collectively act for the greater good.

Chapter 4
Quantum Dynamics - The Dance of the Smallest Particles

In a world dominated by the familiar rules of classical physics, where objects behave in predictable ways, there exists a realm where the rules are fundamentally different—a realm inhabited by the tiniest particles of our universe: atoms, electrons, and photons. This is the world of quantum dynamics, a fascinating and often perplexing area of physics that explores the behaviour of matter and energy at the smallest scales. To understand quantum dynamics is to glimpse the very fabric of reality itself, and its implications stretch far beyond the realms of science into the very core of our future prosperity and survival.

The Nature of Quantum Dynamics

Imagine a tiny particle, like an electron, zooming around in an atom. In classical physics, you might picture it as a small ball following a defined path, much like a planet orbits the sun. However, in the quantum world, things are not so straightforward. Electrons do not have fixed positions or velocities; instead, they exist in a cloud of probabilities. This means that until we observe or measure an electron's position, it can be thought of as existing in multiple places at once. This idea is famously illustrated by the thought experiment known as

Schrödinger's cat, where a cat in a box is both alive and dead until someone opens the box and observes it.

This inherent uncertainty is one of the cornerstones of quantum dynamics, known as the Heisenberg Uncertainty Principle. It tells us that the more accurately we know a particle's position, the less accurately we can know its momentum, and vice versa. This concept challenges our classical intuition and opens the door to a universe that is inherently probabilistic rather than deterministic.

Quantum Superposition and Entanglement

Another intriguing aspect of quantum dynamics is the phenomenon of superposition. This principle states that particles can exist in multiple states simultaneously. Imagine flipping a coin. While it spins in the air, it is neither heads nor tails, but a combination of both until it lands. In the quantum realm, particles can be in a superposition of multiple states at once, which allows for a vast array of possibilities.

Entanglement is another fascinating feature of quantum dynamics, where particles become linked in such a way that the state of one particle instantly influences the state of another, no matter how far apart they are. This peculiar connection defies classical notions of locality and has led scientists to describe entangled particles as being "spooky" at a distance. The implications of entanglement are profound, suggesting that information can be shared instantaneously across vast distances, a concept that challenges our understanding of space and time.

The Scientific Revolution: Quantum Mechanics

The understanding of quantum dynamics has led to a scientific revolution, reshaping our knowledge of the universe. Quantum mechanics, the mathematical framework that describes these phenomena, has enabled breakthroughs in various fields, from chemistry to material science. For instance, the principles of quantum dynamics are crucial in explaining how atoms bond to form molecules, which is fundamental to the development of new materials and pharmaceuticals.

Moreover, quantum dynamics has also given rise to technologies that have transformed our everyday lives. The invention of transistors, lasers, and modern electronics can all be traced back to quantum principles. These advancements have paved the way for the information age, where computing power and connectivity define our society.

Quantum Computing: A New Frontier

As scientists continue to unravel the mysteries of quantum dynamics, one of the most exciting developments on the horizon is quantum computing. Traditional computers rely on bits as the smallest units of information, which can be either 0 or 1. Quantum computers, on the other hand, use qubits—quantum bits that can exist in a state of superposition. This allows quantum computers to process vast amounts of information simultaneously, dramatically increasing their computational power.

Imagine solving complex problems that would take classical computers years or even centuries to crack. Quantum computers could revolutionise fields such as cryptography, optimisation, and drug discovery. For instance, they could simulate molecular interactions with unprecedented accuracy, leading to the development of new medications tailored to specific diseases.

However, the journey to quantum computing is fraught with challenges. Building stable qubits that can maintain their quantum states long enough to perform computations is no small feat. Moreover, the potential for quantum computers to break traditional encryption methods poses significant risks to data security. As we venture into this new frontier, it is crucial to address these challenges and consider the ethical implications of such powerful technologies.

Implications for Human Endeavour

The potential applications of quantum dynamics extend far beyond computing. In energy, quantum principles could lead to the development of more efficient solar cells and batteries, transforming our approach to renewable energy. In communications, quantum entanglement could enable ultra-secure communication networks, safeguarding sensitive information from prying eyes.

Moreover, quantum dynamics offers new insights into the fundamental nature of reality, challenging our philosophical perspectives on existence and consciousness. As we delve deeper into the quantum realm, we begin to ask profound questions about the universe and our place within it. What is the nature of reality? Are we merely observers in a world governed by probabilities? These inquiries push the boundaries of science and philosophy, encouraging interdisciplinary dialogue that could shape our understanding of existence itself.**

Survival and Prosperity: The Importance of Quantum Dynamics

Understanding quantum dynamics is not just an academic pursuit; it has real-world implications for humanity's future. As we confront global challenges such as climate change, resource scarcity, and health crises, the innovations driven by quantum mechanics could provide solutions. For instance, advancements in quantum computing could lead to breakthroughs in materials science that produce more efficient energy sources or improve agricultural practices to feed a growing population.

The ability to model complex systems with quantum computers can enhance our understanding of climate dynamics, allowing for better predictive models that inform policy decisions. In medicine, quantum simulations could enable the rapid development of vaccines and treatments, addressing health crises more effectively than traditional methods.

The Risks

However, with great power comes great responsibility. The exploration of quantum dynamics also presents significant risks and ethical dilemmas. As quantum technologies evolve, we must consider the implications of their misuse. For instance, quantum computing's capability to break conventional encryption could jeopardise sensitive data, leading to breaches of privacy and security.

Moreover, the potential for quantum technologies to exacerbate existing inequalities cannot be ignored. Access to advanced quantum computing resources could become a privilege of wealthy nations and corporations, widening the gap between those with access to cutting-edge technology and those without. This disparity could lead to geopolitical tensions and ethical questions surrounding the ownership and control of quantum innovations.

Navigating the Quantum Future

To navigate the complexities of the quantum future, a multi-faceted approach is essential. Collaboration among scientists, policymakers, ethicists, and the public will be crucial in shaping a framework that ensures the responsible development and deployment of quantum technologies. This includes establishing guidelines for ethical research practices, data privacy, and equitable access to technology.

Education will play a vital role in preparing the next generation to engage with quantum dynamics. By fostering an understanding of the principles of quantum mechanics, we can empower young minds to innovate and contribute to solving the challenges we face. Interdisciplinary education that combines science, philosophy, and ethics will equip future leaders with the tools to navigate the complexities of quantum technologies.

The Journey Ahead

As we stand on the brink of a new era defined by quantum dynamics, we must embrace the unknown with curiosity and caution. The journey ahead is filled with possibilities, but it also requires vigilance and foresight. By harnessing the power of quantum mechanics, we can unlock solutions to some of humanity's most pressing issues while ensuring that the benefits are shared equitably across society.

In conclusion, quantum dynamics is not merely a scientific curiosity; it is a gateway to understanding the universe and a catalyst for innovation that could define our collective future. As we explore this fascinating realm, we must remain mindful of the risks involved, striving to create a world where the advancements driven by quantum mechanics contribute to the prosperity and survival of all. The dance of the smallest particles is a reminder of the interconnectedness of existence, urging us to work together toward a better tomorrow.

Call to Action

To harness the potential of quantum dynamics for the greater good, we must take action now. Advocating for policies that promote research and development in quantum technologies, supporting education initiatives that demystify these concepts, and engaging in public discourse about the ethical implications of our discoveries will pave the way for a brighter future.

As we look to the stars and contemplate the mysteries of the universe, let us remember that the journey into the quantum realm is not just about exploring the unknown; it's about building a sustainable, equitable, and prosperous world for generations to come. The future is quantum, and it is up to us to shape it wisely.

Chapter 5
World Peace 'Hands of Hope'

In a world teetering on the brink of chaos, where the spectre of conflict loomed large, the idea of global peace seemed an elusive dream. Nations, once bound by shared aspirations, had become entangled in a web of power plays, resource competition, and technological arms races. In this story, we explore the intricate tapestry of human relationships, the struggles for dominance, and the quest for a harmonious existence amidst the turmoil.

The year is 2045, and the world has become a patchwork of factions. The United Nations, once a beacon of hope for diplomacy, had fractured into regional blocs, each vying for influence and control. National leaders, driven by ambition and ego, often prioritised their own power over the collective good. The allure of resources—oil, water, rare minerals—fuelled conflicts that erupted in places once known for their beauty and tranquility.

In the heart of this turmoil stood President Selma Janssen of the United Federations, a coalition of nations committed to cooperation. She believed in the power of dialogue and diplomacy, yet her voice was often drowned out by the clamour of militaristic rhetoric. The leaders of rival factions, emboldened by the backing of powerful multinational corporations, saw her ideals as naïve.

As tensions escalated, a new player emerged on the global stage: Star Technologies, a conglomerate known for its advancements in artificial intelligence and weaponry. The CEO, Nole Ksum, saw the potential for profit in conflict and sought to manipulate world leaders to secure lucrative defence contracts. Under his influence, the arms race intensified, as nations scrambled to outdo one another in technological prowess.

In this new world order, military strength and technological superiority became the ultimate currency. Nations invested heavily in research and development, pouring resources into weapons systems that promised to ensure their dominance. But as the race escalated, so too did the risks.

The United Federations, while striving for peace, found itself at a disadvantage. It lacked the financial clout of Star Technologies and the backing of powerful allies. President Janssen understood that true security could not be achieved through weapons alone; it required trust, cooperation, and a shared vision for the future.

Amidst the growing tensions, a summit was convened in Geneva, bringing together the leaders of the most powerful nations. President Janssen seized the opportunity to advocate for disarmament and cooperation.

"We must remember that our greatest strength lies not in our weapons, but in our ability to work together," proclaimed, her voice steady yet passionate.

However, her words fell on deaf ears. The leaders, influenced by their corporate backers, dismissed her vision as impractical. In their eyes, peace was a luxury they could not afford; they were embroiled in a game of survival, where the stakes were measured in power and resources.

As the arms race escalated, so too did the humanitarian crises that plagued the world. Wars raged in regions rich in resources, leaving millions displaced and suffering. Refugee camps swelled with families torn apart by violence, their hopes for a better future dashed by the greed of those in power.

In a small village in the conflict-ridden region of Tijuana, a young girl named Maja dreamed of peace. She witnessed the horrors of war firsthand—her father had been taken by soldiers, and her mother struggled to provide for her and her younger siblings. Maja's heart ached for a world where children could play without fear, where laughter replaced the sounds of gunfire.

One day, while scavenging for food, Maya stumbled upon a group of aid workers from the United Federations. They were distributing supplies and medical care to those in need. Maja approached them, her eyes filled with curiosity and hope. "Will you help us?" she asked, her voice barely a whisper. The aid workers, touched by her courage and resilience, promised to do everything they could. They shared stories of their own struggles and the importance of unity in the face of adversity. Maja felt a flicker of hope ignite within her—a belief that, despite the darkness, there were still those willing to stand for peace.

Back in Geneva, President Janssen refused to give up. She recognised that the key to change lay not only in the hands of leaders but also in the hearts of the people. Inspired by Maja's courage, she launched a global campaign for peace, calling for citizens around the world to unite in their desire for a better future.

The campaign, dubbed "hands of hope," encouraged individuals to share their stories of hope and resilience. Social media platforms buzzed with messages of solidarity, as people from all walks of life joined the movement. Artists created artistic expressions, musicians composed anthems of peace, and writers penned heartfelt letters, all echoing the universal desire for harmony. The movement transcended borders, uniting voices that had long been silenced by the din of conflict.

As the campaign gained momentum, something remarkable began to happen. Citizens from different nations, once perceived as adversaries, started to connect on a personal level. They shared their hopes and dreams, their fears and struggles, and in doing so, they discovered their shared humanity. Maja's story, along with countless others, became a source of inspiration, igniting a flame of compassion that spread like wildfire.

President Janssen recognised the power of this grassroots movement. She arranged for a global peace summit, inviting representatives from every nation, as well as activists, artists, and ordinary citizens who had been touched by the campaign. The goal was not to negotiate treaties or draw borders but to foster understanding and collaboration.

The summit took place in a grand hall adorned with symbols of peace from around the world. As delegates gathered, the atmosphere was charged with a mix of hope and skepticism. Many leaders arrived with their own agendas, still influenced by the corporations that funded their campaigns. However, they were met with an unexpected force: the collective spirit of the people who had rallied for change.

During the summit, President Janssen stood before the assembly, her heart pounding. "We are at a crossroads," she began. "We can continue down the path of division and destruction, or we can choose a different way—a path paved with understanding, compassion, and collaboration."

She urged the leaders to listen to the voices of their citizens, to recognise that true strength lay not in military might but in the ability to unite for a common cause. "We must prioritise the needs of our people over the interests of corporations that profit from conflict," she declared.

As she spoke, testimonials from individuals affected by war were shared on giant screens. Maja's face appeared, her eyes shining with hope as she expressed her longing for a world free from fear. The room fell silent as delegates absorbed the weight of her words. For the first time, many leaders looked around and saw not just representatives of rival nations but fellow human beings capable of empathy and compassion.

Encouraged by the grassroots movement, several leaders began to shift their stances. They acknowledged the need for cooperation in addressing global challenges—climate change, poverty, and health crises—that transcended national borders. The conversation transformed from one of competition to collaboration, with delegates proposing joint initiatives aimed at building a sustainable future.

As the summit progressed, a historic agreement began to take shape. The leaders committed to a framework for disarmament, vowing to reduce military spending and redirect funds toward humanitarian efforts and sustainable development. They agreed to establish an international council dedicated to addressing global crises collaboratively, ensuring that all voices were heard.

In the aftermath of the summit, the world experienced a palpable shift. The media, once focused on conflict and division, began to highlight stories of hope and cooperation. Nations that had been at odds for decades started to engage in dialogues, exploring avenues for collaboration rather than confrontation.

Star Technologies, sensing the changing tides, faced mounting pressure from the public to pivot its focus away from weapons manufacturing. Activists and consumers demanded ethical practices, urging the company to invest in technologies that could address pressing global issues. In response, Nole Ksum found himself at a crossroads; the question of whether to adapt or cling to the past weighed heavily on him.

Despite the progress, challenges remained. The road to peace was fraught with obstacles, as entrenched interests continued to resist change. Some leaders clung to their power and influence, unwilling to relinquish the status quo. In Tijuana, violence erupted once more, fuelled by factions that sought to undermine the peace movement. Maja, now a teenager, watched helplessly as her village was once again torn apart by conflict.

Amidst the turmoil, President Janssen remained resolute. She understood that true peace required not only agreements but a transformation of hearts and minds. She launched an initiative to empower youth like Maja, fostering leadership skills, resilience, and a commitment to advocacy. The program encouraged young people to become ambassadors for peace, equipping them with the tools to effect change in their communities.

Maja eagerly joined the initiative, driven by her desire to make a difference. She participated in workshops, learning about conflict resolution and diplomacy. Inspired by the stories of other young leaders, she began organising community events, bringing together people from different backgrounds to share their experiences and build bridges of understanding.

As Maja's efforts gained traction, a ripple effect spread throughout Tijuana. Her community, once divided by fear and animosity, began to transform. Maja organised peace circles where villagers could come together, share their stories, and discuss their hopes for a better future. The gatherings were simple yet profound, providing a safe space for people to express their feelings and grievances. Over time, former enemies found common ground, discovering shared experiences that united them rather than dividing them.

Word of Maja's initiatives reached neighbouring villages, inspiring similar movements. Young people across Tijuana began to take action, forming their own peace committees. They held workshops, created art that expressed their dreams of unity, and engaged in dialogues with local leaders, urging them to prioritise peace over power.

As these efforts gained momentum, the older generations who had once been entrenched in conflict started to take notice. Many were moved by the determination of the youth, realising that their own beliefs and prejudices were being challenged. Slowly, a cultural shift began to take root, as people recognised the futility of violence and the strength of community.

President Janssen, hearing of the grassroots movements blossoming in Tijuana, decided to visit the region. She addressed the community, sharing her own journey and the power of collective action. "You are the architects of your own future," she proclaimed. "Together, you can build a legacy of peace that will resonate for generations to come."

Her visit galvanised the community, and a new sense of hope emerged. The villagers began to envision a future where cooperation and understanding replaced conflict. They sought to establish a community council that included representatives from all factions, ensuring that every voice was heard and valued.

Back on the international stage, the peace movement continued to gather steam. The success of the grassroots initiatives in Tijuana inspired global leaders to take action. A coalition of nations, united by a shared commitment to peace and cooperation, began to develop policies that prioritised humanitarian aid, education, and sustainable development.

With the support of multinational corporations willing to pivot their focus, innovative solutions to global challenges began to emerge. Star Technologies, under pressure from activists and the public, announced a new initiative to develop technologies aimed at addressing climate change and improving access to clean water. Nole Ksum, having witnessed the power of collective action, recognised that the future lay not in conflict, but in collaboration.

As countries worked together to address pressing issues, the narrative surrounding global relations shifted. The focus moved from competition and rivalry to partnership and shared responsibility. Nations that had once been adversaries collaborated on initiatives to combat poverty, improve education, and promote healthcare.

The UN, revitalised by this newfound spirit of cooperation, re-emerged as a central player in fostering global dialogue. With the involvement of civil society and grassroots movements, the organisation began to prioritise the voices of the people, ensuring that the needs of the vulnerable were at the forefront of decision-making.

Years passed, and the world began to see the fruits of its labour. In Tijuana, Maja grew into a young leader, continuing her work to promote peace and understanding. The village that had once been torn apart by conflict became a model for reconciliation, inspiring neighbouring regions to adopt similar approaches.

The international landscape had changed dramatically. Conflicts that once seemed intractable were now being resolved through dialogue and diplomacy. Disarmament agreements became a reality, as nations dedicated themselves to reducing their arsenals in favour of collaborative projects that benefited all.

The global community celebrated significant milestones—hunger rates decreased, access to education expanded, and health outcomes improved. The spirit of unity was palpable, as people from diverse backgrounds found common ground.

Yet, Maja understood that the journey toward lasting peace was ongoing. Challenges remained, and the threat of division still loomed. She continued to advocate for education and empowerment, believing that the key to sustaining peace lay in the hands of the next generation.

As Maja prepared to address a gathering of young leaders from around the world, she reflected on the journey that had brought them to this moment. The auditorium was filled with passionate voices, each representing a unique story of resilience and hope. Maja felt a surge of gratitude for the collective efforts that had paved the way for a brighter future.

Taking the stage, she began her address: "Today, we stand on the shoulders of those who came before us—those who fought for peace, who believed in the power of unity. Let us honour their legacy by continuing to build bridges, by fostering understanding, and by embracing our shared humanity."

The audience erupted in applause, their energy infectious. Maja's words resonated deeply, igniting a commitment to carry the torch of peace forward.

As the conference concluded, Maja and her peers brainstormed ways to expand their initiatives, envisioning a world where every child could grow up free from fear and violence. They dreamed of a global network of youth ambassadors dedicated to peace, each equipped with the tools and knowledge to enact change in their communities. This coalition would harness the power of social media, art, and grassroots activism to amplify their voices and inspire others to join their cause.

As they brainstormed, the room buzzed with ideas. Maja suggested organising a global day of action where young people could participate in simultaneous events advocating for peace, justice, and sustainability. The idea was met with enthusiasm, and soon, plans were set in motion for a worldwide event that would unite voices across continents.

They envisioned a day filled with educational workshops, art exhibitions, and cultural exchanges that would celebrate diversity while promoting understanding. The initiative would not only raise awareness, but also empower young people to take an active role in shaping their futures.

Months later, the global day of action arrived. Cities around the world erupted with vibrant displays of creativity and solidarity. In Tijuana, Maja and her peers organised a festival in the village square, complete with music, dance, and storytelling. Villagers of all ages came together, sharing their experiences and celebrating their journey toward reconciliation.

Meanwhile, in urban centres, youth-led events took place in parks, schools, and community centres. They hosted discussions on peace-building, invited local leaders to share their experiences, and engaged in collaborative art projects that expressed their visions for a harmonious future. Social media buzzed with hashtags promoting the event, creating a virtual tapestry of voices advocating for change.

As the day unfolded, a sense of hope permeated the atmosphere. Maja received messages of support from youth ambassadors across the globe, sharing pictures and stories of their own events. The collective energy was palpable, a testament to the power of unity and shared purpose.

In the aftermath of the global day of action, the momentum continued to build. Media outlets covered the event extensively, showcasing the stories of young leaders like Maja who were driving change in their communities. The world began to take notice of the transformative power of grassroots movements, leading to increased support for initiatives aimed at fostering peace and cooperation.

Policymakers, inspired by the energy of the youth, began to engage more actively with civil society. They recognised that the voices of young people were not only important, but essential in shaping policies that would affect their futures. Collaborative forums were established to facilitate dialogue between youth leaders and decision-makers, ensuring that the aspirations of the next generation were heard and considered.

In Tijuana, the community council that Maja had helped establish began to gain traction. It became a platform for addressing local issues and fostering collaboration among residents. The council organised workshops to tackle challenges such as education access, economic development, and environmental sustainability, empowering citizens to take ownership of their community's future.

While progress was evident, Maja knew that the journey was far from over. Global challenges remained—climate change, inequality, and persistent conflicts that threatened the hard-won gains of the past few years. She understood that sustaining peace required vigilance, commitment, and a willingness to adapt.

Maja and her peers continued their advocacy, participating in international conferences and collaborating with organisations working toward social justice. They sought to amplify the voices of marginalised communities, ensuring that every perspective was considered in the pursuit of peace.

Through workshops and mentorship programs, Maja inspired young people to become change-makers in their own right. She encouraged them to harness their passions—whether in art, science, or activism—to contribute to the broader movement for peace. The ripple effect of their efforts reached far beyond Tijuana, as youth across the globe began to see themselves as agents of change.

Years later, as Maja stood before a crowd at an international summit focused on youth empowerment, she reflected on the journey that had brought her to this moment. The room was filled with young leaders from different cultures and backgrounds, all united by a common goal: to create a more just and peaceful world.

"Together, we have the power to shape our future," Maja addressed the audience, her voice steady with conviction. "Let us continue to build on the legacy of those who fought for peace before us. Let us be the change-makers, the dreamers, and the doers. Our voices are our greatest weapon against division and despair."

The audience erupted in applause, their enthusiasm a testament to the collective hope that permeated the air. Maja felt a surge of determination as she looked around the room, recognising that the future was bright with possibilities.

In the years that followed, the world witnessed a shift toward a more collaborative and empathetic society. The lessons learned from the grassroots movements, the importance of dialogue, and the power of youth advocacy became integral to the fabric of international relations.

Chapter 6
The Life and Legacy of Nikola Tesla

Early Life and Awakening

In the small village of Smiljan, nestled within the mountainous terrain of what is now Croatia, a prodigy was born on July 10, 1856. Nikola Tesla, the fourth of five children, showed signs of extraordinary intelligence from a young age. He was fascinated by the natural world, often spending hours exploring the fields and forests surrounding his home. His mother, a talented inventor of household tools, inspired young Nikola's love for invention, while his father, a strict priest, hoped for his son to follow in his religious footsteps.

As a child, Tesla was plagued by vivid dreams and hallucinations, experiences that would later inform his understanding of creativity and invention. He often described these visions as a form of meditation—a way to tap into the boundless well of inspiration that lay within him. This practice allowed him to visualise inventions with such clarity that he could mentally construct and test them before ever setting them down on paper.

Tesla's formal education began at the Polytechnic Institute in Graz, Austria, where he excelled in physics and mathematics. However, his insatiable thirst for knowledge often led him to clash with professors who adhered to traditional scientific paradigms. After a brief stint at the university, he left without a degree, but not without a burning desire to change the world through electricity.

The Spark of Genius: Significant Inventions

In 1881, Tesla moved to Budapest, where he began working for the Central Telephone Exchange. It was here that he proposed the idea of the induction motor, a revolutionary concept that would enable the use of alternating current (AC) electricity. This marked the beginning of a series of significant inventions that would define his legacy.

In 1884, Tesla emigrated to the United States, landing in New York City with little more than a few cents and a letter of recommendation to Thomas Edison. Tesla's brief partnership with Edison was fraught with conflict. Edison, a staunch proponent of direct current (DC), dismissed Tesla's AC ideas. Their differing visions culminated in a bitter rivalry known as the "War of Currents," which played out publicly as each inventor sought to prove the superiority of their electrical systems.

Tesla's most notable inventions include the Tesla coil, a high-voltage transformer that produces spectacular electrical discharges; the polyphase AC motor, which laid the groundwork for modern electric power distribution; and the radio, for which he laid the theoretical foundations, although credit was controversially claimed by Guglielmo Marconi. Each invention was a manifestation of Tesla's unique vision—an effort to harness and distribute electricity in ways that could empower humanity.

The Tesla coil, in particular, stands out not only for its technical prowess but also for its theatrical demonstrations. Tesla would illuminate bulbs wirelessly and create mesmerising arcs of electricity that danced in the air, captivating audiences and inspiring future generations of scientists and inventors.

The Power of Meditation and Creativity

Tesla's ability to visualise and innovate was deeply intertwined with his meditative practices. He believed that the mind could be harnessed to reach higher states of consciousness, enabling the flow of creativity. In his later years, Tesla became increasingly reclusive, often retreating into solitude to meditate and contemplate his next grand idea.

His meditative state allowed him to explore concepts beyond the physical realm. He envisioned wireless transmission of energy and even dreamed of harnessing the power of the Earth itself. Tesla's imagination knew no bounds; he famously claimed to have received ideas from a higher source, which he described as a "vibrational frequency" that connected him with the universe.

However, such lofty ideas often led to frustration. Many of Tesla's inventions, though groundbreaking, were not commercialised. The world was not yet ready for wireless power transmission, and investors were hesitant to back projects that seemed too far-fetched. Tesla's visions often outpaced the technological capabilities of his time, leading to a disconnect between his genius and practical application.

The Fall from Grace

Despite his remarkable contributions to science, Tesla struggled with financial instability throughout his life. He was a man of ideals, often prioritising invention over profit. His pursuit of knowledge and innovation left little room for the business acumen necessary to secure his inventions' commercial success.

In 1893, Tesla held a demonstration in St. Louis at the World's Fair, showcasing his wireless lighting technology. While the event garnered significant attention, it did not translate into financial support. Tesla's later ventures, including the construction of the Wardenclyffe Tower, aimed to create a global wireless communication system, but were met with skepticism and ultimately led to bankruptcy.

His financial troubles were exacerbated by his relationships with investors and industrialists who were more interested in short-term profits than in supporting Tesla's visionary projects. J.P. Morgan, who financed the Wardenclyffe project, withdrew his support when Tesla's ideas.

The Struggles of a Visionary

As Tesla's financial situation deteriorated, his once-thriving laboratories became shadows of their former glory. While his contemporaries, like Edison and Westinghouse, basked in wealth and public acclaim, Tesla found himself increasingly isolated. His eccentric nature, coupled with his disdain for the commercial aspects of invention, alienated potential investors. Tesla's insistence on pursuing projects that he deemed beneficial for humanity often meant sacrificing immediate financial gain, leading to a series of failed partnerships and business ventures.

The pinnacle of his struggles came with the downfall of the Wardenclyffe Tower project. Tesla envisioned the tower as a means to transmit wireless communication and power across vast distances. It symbolised his dream of a world where energy was freely available to all, unrestricted by the limitations of wires and infrastructure. However, as construction progressed, it became increasingly clear that the project was not going to yield immediate returns. J.P. Morgan, initially intrigued by Tesla's vision, became disillusioned when it became apparent that the technology was not ready for commercialisation.

In 1906, after years of hard work, the Wardenclyffe Tower was dismantled due to financial insolvency. This represented a personal and professional failure for Tesla, but rather than succumb to despair, he continued to innovate. He remained devoted to his ideas, even as the world around him seemed to overlook his brilliance.

The Twilight Years

In the years that followed, Tesla lived in relative obscurity, often residing in hotels and relying on small speaking engagements and royalties from his patents to get by. The great inventor who had once dazzled the world with his demonstrations of electricity now found solace in solitude. Though he remained active in his scientific pursuits, his ideas became increasingly radical and unconventional, leading many to label him as a mad scientist.

Despite the decline of his physical and financial health, Tesla's mind remained sharp. He continued to publish articles and give lectures, advocating for renewable energy sources and the potential of harnessing natural forces. He even foresaw technologies that would later emerge, such as smartphones and wireless internet. In his mind, he was still a pioneer of the future, but the world had moved on, and his groundbreaking ideas were often dismissed as fanciful dreams.

In his later years, Tesla's eccentricities became more pronounced. He claimed to have developed a "death ray," a device that could project concentrated beams of energy capable of destroying enemy aircraft. While he sought funding for this invention during the tumultuous years leading to World War II, the scientific community regarded his claims with skepticism, and funding remained elusive. Ironically, some of the military technologies developed during the war echoed ideas Tesla had proposed years earlier.

The Legacy of Tesla

Nikola Tesla passed away on January 7, 1943, in a modest hotel room in New York City, alone and impoverished. His death marked the end of a remarkable life filled with creativity and brilliance, but it also served as a poignant reminder of the often-unrecognised contributions of visionary thinkers. He had died without the wealth and recognition that many of his contemporaries enjoyed, yet his impact on the world of science and technology would be felt for generations to come.

In the years following his death, Tesla's legacy began to be rediscovered and celebrated. His contributions to the development of alternating current power systems became foundational to modern electrical engineering.

The Tesla coil, once a simple demonstration of electrical prowess, found applications in various fields, including radio broadcasting and medical technology.

Moreover, as the world transitioned to a more sustainable future, Tesla's ideas about harnessing renewable energy and wireless transmission gained renewed interest. The advent of wireless communication, smartphones, and the internet echoed the visionary concepts he had proposed a century earlier. Tesla's name slowly became synonymous with innovation and creativity, and his life story transformed into an inspiring narrative for inventors and dreamers alike.

The Reclamation of a Hero

Today, Tesla is celebrated not only for his inventions but also for his relentless pursuit of knowledge and his commitment to the betterment of humanity. Numerous institutions, awards, and even electric vehicles bear his name, serving as a testament to his enduring influence. Museums dedicated to his life and work have sprung up, showcasing his inventions and celebrating his genius.

Tesla's story serves as a powerful reminder of the complexities of innovation, the struggles of creative minds, and the often-unseen battles waged in the pursuit of progress. He epitomises the archetype of the misunderstood genius, whose ideas were often far ahead of their time. His life encourages us to recognise the value of creativity and to embrace the visionaries who dare to dream.

The Eternal Flame of Innovation

Nikola Tesla may have left this world as a pauper, but his legacy is rich with inspiration and innovation. His life was characterised by a deep passion for discovery and a commitment to harnessing the forces of nature for the benefit of humanity.

Chapter 7
The Symphony of Resonance

Ancient Understanding of Sound

From the earliest days of human civilisation, sound has played a vital role in cultural and spiritual practices. Ancient civilisations recognised the profound effects that sound and vibration could have on the human mind and body. The concept of resonance—where one vibrating object causes another object to vibrate at the same frequency—was not just a scientific phenomenon, but a spiritual and healing principle that informed their rituals and practices.

In ancient Egypt, for instance, sound was deeply woven into the fabric of their religious and healing practices. The priests, known as "healers," used specific sounds during their rituals to invoke divine presence and facilitate healing. They employed instruments like the sistrum—a sacred rattle that produced a resonant sound believed to appease the goddess Hathor, associated with music, dance, and healing. The vibrations created by the sistrum were thought to resonate with the divine and promote harmony within the body, mind, and spirit.

Across the Mediterranean in ancient Greece, philosophers like Pythagoras explored the mathematical basis of musical harmony. Pythagoras believed that the universe was governed by mathematical ratios and that music could influence not only emotions, but also physical health. He established the concept of "Music of the Spheres," suggesting that celestial bodies produced a unique sound based on their movements. This cosmic resonance was thought to have a direct effect on the human spirit, promoting healing and balance.

Resonance in Eastern Traditions

In the East, the understanding of sound as a healing force took on a different form but was equally profound. Traditional Indian healing practices, particularly Ayurveda, emphasised the use of sound and vibration for both physical and spiritual well-being. The chanting of mantras, such as "Om," was believed to create vibrational frequencies that align the body's energies and promote healing.

The practice of sound therapy in Buddhism also played a significant role in meditation and healing. Tibetan singing bowls, made from a mix of metals, are used to produce harmonic sounds that resonate with the body's energy centres, or chakras. When struck or rubbed, these bowls emit a rich, sonorous tone that can induce deep relaxation and heightened states of awareness. Practitioners believe that the vibrations produced by the bowls help clear energetic blockages, facilitating healing on a physical, emotional, and spiritual level.

Moving Heavy Objects with Sound

The ancient Egyptians and other civilisations also demonstrated a remarkable understanding of resonance in their construction techniques. There are theories suggesting that sound was used to move heavy stones during the construction of monumental structures like the pyramids. Although the exact methods remain a subject of speculation, some researchers propose that specific frequencies could create vibrations strong enough to lift or move large blocks of stone.

One prominent theory posits that by creating a resonant frequency that matched the natural vibration of the stones, workers could reduce friction and make the stones easier to manipulate. This principle of resonance suggests that everything in the universe has a frequency, and by aligning with that frequency, one can affect the physical properties of matter. While conclusive evidence remains elusive, the idea that sound could have been used to manipulate heavy objects reflects an advanced understanding of physics by ancient cultures.

The Evolution of Sound Healing

As civilisations evolved, so did the understanding and application of sound for healing. The ancient Greeks, with their emphasis on harmony and proportion, contributed to the development of music therapy. By the time of the Renaissance, music was viewed as a powerful tool for healing the soul and body. The concept of "music as medicine" gained traction, with physicians prescribing specific types of music to alleviate ailments.

In the 19th century, the advent of scientific inquiry led to a more structured approach to sound therapy. Pioneers like Dr. Alfred Tomatis explored the effects of sound on the brain. He developed the Tomatis Method, which used sound to stimulate auditory processing and improve cognitive functions. This marked the beginning of a more empirical approach to understanding the healing properties of sound.

Resonance in Modern Medicine

The 20th century saw a renaissance in the study of resonance in medicine. Researchers began to explore the concept of bioresonance, a technique that utilises the frequencies of the body's cells to diagnose and treat illness. Bioresonance therapy operates on the principle that every cell in the body emits a specific frequency and that imbalances in these frequencies can lead to health issues.

Modern bioresonance machines analyse the frequencies emitted by the body and identify areas of disharmony. The therapy then employs electromagnetic frequencies to restore balance, allowing the body to heal itself. This approach has gained traction in alternative medicine, with practitioners claiming success in treating various conditions, including chronic pain, allergies, and even emotional disorders.

Modern therapeutic practices utilise sound in various innovative ways to promote healing and well-being. Here are some common methods:

Music Therapy

This involves the use of music by trained therapists to address emotional, cognitive, and social needs. It can help reduce anxiety, improve mood, and enhance communication skills, especially in individuals with developmental disorders or mental health issues.

Sound Bath

Participants are immersed in sound generated by various instruments, such as Tibetan singing bowls, gongs, and chimes. The vibrations and harmonics aim to promote relaxation, reduce stress, and enhance mindfulness.

Binaural Beats

This technique uses two slightly different frequencies played in each ear, creating a perceived third frequency in the brain. It is believed to help with relaxation, meditation, and even sleep improvement by promoting brainwave entrainment.

Tuning Fork Therapy

Practitioners use tuning forks to apply specific frequencies to various points on the body. This method is thought to stimulate energy flow and promote healing by balancing the body's vibrational frequencies.

Chanting and Mantra Recitation

Used in various spiritual and meditation practices, chanting specific sounds or mantras can help focus the mind, reduce stress, and enhance spiritual connection.

Sound Frequencies in Physiotherapy

Ultrasonic sound waves are used in physical therapy to promote healing in soft tissues, reduce pain, and improve circulation.

Voice and Sound Healing

Practitioners use their voice to create specific sounds or tones, which are believed to resonate with the body's energy centres, promoting emotional and physical healing.

Environmental Sound Therapy

The use of natural sounds, like flowing water or birdsong, in therapeutic settings can help reduce stress, improve mood, and enhance relaxation.

These practices harness the power of sound to foster physical, emotional, and spiritual well-being, reflecting an ancient understanding of resonance and its healing potential.

Using music in therapy sessions offers a wide range of benefits, including:

Emotional Expression

Music provides a safe outlet for clients to express their feelings, enabling them to process emotions that may be difficult to articulate verbally.

Stress Reduction

Listening to or creating music can lower stress levels, decrease anxiety, and promote relaxation, helping clients feel more at ease during therapy.

Enhanced Communication

Music can facilitate communication, especially for individuals with speech or language challenges. It can help bridge gaps in communication, making it easier to connect and share thoughts.

Improved Mood

Engaging with music can elevate mood and foster positive feelings, which can be particularly beneficial for individuals dealing with depression or emotional distress.

Cognitive Stimulation

Music therapy can enhance cognitive functioning, improving memory, attention, and problem-solving skills, particularly in individuals with cognitive impairments.

Social Connection

Group music therapy fosters a sense of community and belonging, helping clients develop social skills and build relationships with others.

Pain Management

Music has been shown to reduce the perception of pain and can be used as a complementary approach in pain management strategies.

Motivation and Engagement

Incorporating music into therapy can increase client motivation and engagement, making the therapeutic process more enjoyable and effective.

Mindfulness and Presence

Music encourages mindfulness, helping clients stay present in the moment and focus on their experiences, which can enhance self-awareness and reflection.

Cultural and Personal Relevance

Music can be tailored to reflect clients' cultural backgrounds and personal preferences, making therapy more relatable and meaningful.

Overall, music therapy harnesses the emotional, cognitive, and social power of music to support healing and personal growth, making it a valuable tool in therapeutic settings.

The Study of Colour - A Guide to Chromatics

Colours can also have a significant impact on mood and behaviour, influencing emotions, perceptions, and even physiological responses. Here are some potential effects of different colours and how they're symbolic meanings by culture.

These additional associations highlight the rich and diverse meanings that colours can hold across different cultures, reflecting their unique values, beliefs, and traditions.

Red

Often associated with energy, passion, and excitement, red can increase heart rates and stimulate feelings of intensity. It may evoke strong emotions, both positive and negative, and is often used to grab attention.

China - symbolises good luck, happiness, and prosperity; commonly used in celebrations like weddings and the Lunar New Year.

India - represents purity, fertility, and love; red is often worn by brides on their wedding day.

Western Cultures - often associated with passion, danger, or anger.

Blue

Typically linked to calmness and tranquility, blue can promote feelings of peace and relaxation. It is often considered a soothing colour that may help reduce stress and anxiety.

Middle East - often regarded as a protective colour, believed to ward off evil spirits.

Western Cultures - associated with calmness, trust, and stability; commonly used in corporate branding.

India - an symbolise the divine and is associated with Lord Krishna.

Yellow

Associated with happiness and optimism, yellow can stimulate feelings of cheerfulness and joy. However, excessive use may lead to feelings of agitation or frustration.

Japan - represents courage and bravery; yellow is also associated with the emperor in historical contexts.

India - symbolises knowledge, learning, and is often associated with the spring festival of Basant Panchami.

Western Cultures - often linked to happiness, warmth, and optimism.

Green

Representing nature, growth, and harmony, green is often perceived as a calming colour. It can promote feelings of balance, renewal, and relaxation, making it a popular choice in environments aimed at fostering well-being.

Islamic Cultures - sacred colour representing paradise and often associated with the Prophet Muhammad.

Western Cultures - typically symbolises nature, growth, and renewal; can also represent jealousy (e.g., "green with envy").

African Cultures - often associated with fertility and prosperity.

Orange

A vibrant and energetic colour, orange can evoke feelings of enthusiasm and creativity. It is often associated with warmth and friendliness, encouraging social interaction.

Buddhism - sacred colour representing humility and the monastic lifestyle; often worn by monks.

Netherlands - national colour, symbolising Dutch pride and identity, especially during national holidays.

India - represents warmth and vibrancy; associated with festivals and celebrations.

Purple

Often linked to spirituality and luxury, purple can inspire creativity and introspection. It may evoke feelings of calmness and reflection but can also be associated with mystery.

Western Cultures - traditionally associated with royalty, luxury, and wealth; historically difficult to produce, making it rare.

Thailand - the colour of mourning for widows; often worn by women who have lost their husbands.

Brazil - associated with spirituality and the divine.

Pink

Associated with love, compassion, and nurturing, pink can have a calming effect and promote feelings of warmth and comfort. It is often used in environments meant to create a sense of safety and care.

Brown

Representing stability and reliability, brown can evoke feelings of comfort and security. It is often seen as a grounding colour that fosters a sense of connection to nature.

Native American Cultures - represents the earth, stability, and a connection to nature.

Japanese Culture - associated with simplicity and humility, often seen in traditional crafts and aesthetics.

Western Cultures - can symbolise comfort, reliability, and a down-to-earth nature.

Black

While often associated with sophistication and elegance, black can also evoke feelings of sadness or emptiness. Its impact can vary significantly based on context and cultural associations.

Western Cultures - often associated with mourning, death, and formality; also linked to power and elegance.

African Cultures - can symbolise maturity and masculinity; in some contexts, it represents the earth and fertility.

Japan - traditionally associated with formality and elegance, often worn during ceremonies.

White

Symbolising purity and cleanliness, white can create a sense of openness and clarity. However, it may also evoke feelings of emptiness or isolation if overused.

Western Cultures - symbolises purity, innocence, and cleanliness; commonly worn by brides at weddings.

China and India - associated with mourning and death; often worn at funerals.

Japan - represents purity and simplicity; white is also worn during traditional Shinto weddings.

Gold

Egypt - symbolises eternity and the divine, often associated with the gods and the afterlife.

India - represents wealth, prosperity, and success; commonly used in religious ceremonies and festivals.

Western Cultures - associated with luxury, achievement, and high status.

Silver

Native American Cultures - often symbolises intuition and clarity, as well as the moon and feminine energy.

China - associated with wealth and prosperity; silver jewellery is considered auspicious.

Western Cultures - represents elegance and sophistication, often used in awards and recognitions.

Turquoise

Native American Cultures - represents protection and healing, often used in jewellery and sacred objects.

Middle Eastern Cultures - associated with luck and protection against evil; commonly seen in decorative arts.

Chinese Culture - can symbolise tranquility and emotional balance.

Pink

Western Cultures - often associated with femininity, love, and tenderness; used in branding and marketing targeted at women.

Japan - represents spring and renewal, particularly associated with cherry blossoms (sakura).

South African Cultures - can symbolise hope and healing, particularly in the context of breast cancer awareness.

Grey

Western Cultures - often associated with neutrality, balance, and sophistication, but can also symbolise indecision or ambiguity.

Japanese Culture - can represent humility and modesty, often seen in traditional clothing.

African Cultures - may symbolise wisdom and maturity, often associated with elders.

Beige

Western Cultures - represents neutrality, calmness, and simplicity; often used in interior design for a soothing effect.

Middle Eastern Cultures - can symbolise warmth and comfort, often seen in traditional textiles and clothing.

Lavender

Western Cultures - associated with tranquility, spirituality, and femininity; often used in aromatherapy and relaxation practices.

French Culture - represents romance and is commonly associated with the lavender fields of Provence.

Overall, the effects of colour on mood and behaviour can vary greatly depending on individual perceptions, cultural backgrounds, and personal experiences. However, understanding these associations can be beneficial in creating environments that promote desired emotional responses.

Chapter 8
Mind-Over-Matter

"Mind-over-matter" is a phrase that suggests the power of the mind or consciousness to influence or control physical reality. It implies that one's thoughts, beliefs, and mental state can have a significant impact on their physical well-being, performance, and overall life experiences.

The concept of mind-over-matter has been explored in various fields, including philosophy, psychology, and spirituality. Here are some key aspects and interpretations of mind over matter:

Mental Influence on Health

The mind can play a crucial role in influencing physical health and well-being. Positive thoughts, beliefs, and attitudes have been associated with improved immune function, faster recovery from illnesses, and better overall health outcomes. On the other hand, negative thoughts and stress can contribute to the development or exacerbation of physical ailments.

Performance Enhancement

The power of the mind is often emphasised in sports and performance-related activities. Athletes, for example, use techniques such as visualisation, positive affirmations, and mental rehearsal to enhance their performance and achieve their goals. By harnessing their mental focus and mindset, individuals can overcome physical limitations and achieve higher levels of success.

Emotional Regulation

The mind has the ability to regulate emotions and influence one's emotional well-being. By cultivating a positive mindset and adopting techniques such as mindfulness and cognitive-behavioural therapy (CBT), individuals can manage their emotions more effectively and improve their overall mental health. This was something I learned, whilst recovering from my first episode of bipolar.

Law of Attraction

The concept of mind over matter is sometimes associated with the Law of Attraction, which suggests that positive or negative thoughts and beliefs can attract corresponding experiences or outcomes into one's life. According to this perspective, focusing on positive thoughts and beliefs can manifest positive experiences and desired outcomes.

Spiritual and Metaphysical Interpretations

Mind-over-matter is also explored in spiritual and metaphysical teachings. Some belief systems suggest that the mind or consciousness is fundamental and has the power to create and shape physical reality. These teachings often emphasise the importance of aligning one's thoughts, beliefs, and intentions with their desired outcomes.

It's important to note that while the power of the mind is recognised, it should not be seen as a replacement for professional medical advice. Physical health conditions often require appropriate medical intervention, and mental health issues may require therapeutic support. Mind-over-matter should be seen as a complementary approach to overall well-being, working in conjunction with other practices and interventions.

Chapter 9
Focus To Infinity

'Focus to Infinity' is a compelling concept that encapsulates the power of collective consciousness and the potential it holds in overcoming life's hurdles. It is not merely a philosophical idea, but a practical approach to tackling problems and addressing challenges.

At the nucleus of this idea is the belief that every individual mind is a powerhouse of thoughts, ideas, and solutions. It is a wellspring of creativity and innovation. When multiple minds come together, their combined potential is magnified exponentially, creating an infinite reservoir of problem-solving capabilities. This is the essence of the 'Focus to Infinity' concept.

In the context of overcoming life's challenges, this concept is not merely relevant but necessary. In our rapidly changing world, individual capabilities, while significant, are often insufficient. Our challenges are complex and multifaceted; they require diverse perspectives, a multitude of skills, and a collective determination to overcome. 'Focus to Infinity' embodies this collective effort. It encourages us to pool our mental resources, cooperate, collaborate, and conquer our shared problems.

Moreover, this concept underscores the importance of unity and interdependence. It emphasises that while each of us is unique, our combined strengths and collective willpower can make us invincible. Each individual's ideas, when combined with others, can generate solutions that no single mind could have conceived. This is the essence of collective power.

'Focus to Infinity' is not just about solving problems, though. It is also about creating a positive and supportive environment for growth and development. It fosters a culture of inclusivity, where each individual feels valued, heard, and encouraged to contribute. This, in turn, fuels creativity, innovation, and resilience, further strengthening the collective power of the group.

The power of teamwork in sports, or any field for that matter, is undeniable. This stems from the fact that each player or member of a team bringing unique skills, perspectives, and strengths to the table. When these diverse abilities are harmoniously combined, they form a robust and dynamic force capable of achieving shared objectives.

The most successful groups set themselves apart with their ability to skilfully execute a strategy. But what does this mean? It means that every member understands their role within the team and performs it to the best of their ability. The team's strategy serves as a roadmap, guiding each member towards the end goal. This collective understanding and coordinated effort lead to a smooth execution of the plan.

However, the ability to adapt to changing circumstances is equally essential. In sports, for instance, opposing teams often change their tactics mid-game. Weather conditions might alter, or a key player might be injured. In these situations, the team's ability to swiftly adjust their strategy and respond effectively becomes vital.

Adaptability in a team comes from a strong foundation of trust, communication, and mutual respect. When these elements are present, team members feel safe expressing their ideas, which can lead to innovative solutions to sudden problems. Moreover, a team that can adapt quickly is resilient. They do not let setbacks deter them; instead, they use these challenges as stepping stones towards their goal.

In conclusion, 'Focus to Infinity' is a testament to the power of collective consciousness. It underscores the potential that lies within each of us and the infinite possibilities that arise when we combine our strengths. It is a call to action for all of us to come together, share our ideas, and work collaboratively to overcome life's challenges. It is a reminder of the infinite power that lies within our collective minds and the incredible feats we can achieve when we focus our energies together.

Chapter 10
Listening Blind Spot

Listening is a critical skill that often goes under appreciated and under utilised in our bustling world. It holds the key to understanding, empowers us to build strong relationships, and is integral to effective communication. However, most people, unknowingly, suffer from a 'listening blind spot,' a phenomenon that hinders the true comprehension of what is being communicated.

The 'listening blind spot' refers to the common tendency to hear words without truly understanding the intent behind them. It is the gap between hearing and understanding, where the essence of the message often gets lost. This blind spot can cause misinterpretations, confusion, and even conflict, affecting personal and professional relationships.

This reality is further complicated by the fact that communication is not limited to spoken or written words. A significant portion of our communication is non-verbal, transmitted through facial expressions, body language, tone of voice, and even pauses. These non-verbal cues often carry more weight than the actual words spoken. However, many of us, preoccupied with our own thoughts or biases, fail to recognise and interpret these signals accurately.

Active listening is the antidote to the 'listening blind spot.' It involves not only hearing the words being spoken, but also observing the speaker's body language, tone of voice, and other non-verbal cues. It requires us to put aside our own thoughts, judgments, and distractions to truly focus on the speaker. This level of attentiveness allows us to understand the complete message, both verbal and non-verbal, thereby eliminating the listening blind spot.

Moreover, active listening fosters empathy. When we listen with the intent to understand, we are better able to relate to the speaker's emotions and perspectives. This empathy can strengthen our relationships, promote open dialogue, and cultivate a deeper understanding of those around us.

Furthermore, active listening can greatly enhance our learning and problem-solving abilities. By fully engaging in the listening process, we can absorb new information more effectively, comprehend complex ideas, and develop innovative solutions.

Cultural and language barriers can significantly impede effective communication, often leading to misunderstandings and conflicts. They can create several obstacles, some of which are outlined as follows:

Misinterpretation

Different languages have different structures, idioms, and nuances. Even when the language is translated correctly, the underlying intention can be lost. This can lead to misinterpretations and confusion.

Non-Verbal Misunderstandings

Non-verbal communication forms a significant part of our interactions. Gestures, facial expressions, and body language can have different meanings in different cultures. What is considered polite in one culture might be seen as rude or offensive in another.

Stereotyping and Prejudice

Cultural barriers often lead to stereotyping and prejudice. People might make assumptions about others based on their cultural background, which can hinder open and fair communication.

Ethnocentrism

This refers to the belief that one's own culture is superior to others. Such a mindset can lead to a lack of respect and understanding for other cultures, thereby obstructing effective communication.

Difficulty in Expressing Ideas

For non-native speakers, it can be challenging to express complex ideas or emotions in a second language. This can lead to frustration and a lack of effective communication.

Lack of Trust and Understanding

Cultural and language barriers can foster a sense of alienation and misunderstanding. This can lead to a lack of trust, which is a vital component of effective communication.

High Context vs Low Context Cultures

Some cultures rely heavily on implicit communication and context (high context), while others depend on explicit, direct communication (low context). Misunderstandings can occur when people from these different types of cultures interact.

Loss of Critical Information

Critical information can be lost in translation or when non-native speakers lack complete fluency.

Ineffective Business Negotiation

In business scenarios, cultural and language barriers can lead to miscommunication and misunderstandings, which can hinder successful negotiations and collaborations.

Overcoming these barriers requires cultural sensitivity, patience, open-mindedness, and a willingness to learn and adapt. It may involve learning new languages, understanding different cultural practices, and adopting inclusive and respectful communication styles. There are several barriers to active listening that can hinder effective communication. Here are some examples and ways to potentially overcome them:

Distractions

Distractions, both internal and external, can prevent us from actively listening. To overcome this, practice mindfulness to stay focused on the conversation and reduce distractions. If you are in a noisy environment, try to move the conversation to a quieter location.

Prejudgments

We often enter conversations with preconceived notions or biases, which can prevent us from truly understanding the other person's perspective. Try to enter each conversation with an open mind, setting aside judgments and being open to new ideas.

Emotional Reactions

Sometimes, strong emotional reactions can prevent us from listening effectively. If a topic is emotionally charged, it may be helpful to take a moment to calm down and process your emotions before continuing the conversation.

Poor Listening Habits

Some people have a habit of interrupting, not making eye contact, or not providing feedback, all of which can hinder active listening. To overcome this, practice good listening habits such as nodding in agreement, maintaining eye contact, and providing feedback when appropriate.

Information Overload

In today's fast-paced world, we are often bombarded with information, which can make it difficult to focus and listen actively. To manage this, prioritise your conversations and give your full attention to the person speaking.

Physical Barriers

Hearing impairments or physical distance can also be barriers to active listening. Overcome these by using hearing aids if necessary, or utilising technology like video calls to close the physical distance.

Multitasking

Trying to do multiple things at once can prevent active listening. To overcome this, focus solely on the conversation at hand and avoid multitasking.

Lack of Interest

If the subject matter doesn't interest you, it can be challenging to listen actively. Try to find a point of connection or interest in the conversation to help engage your attention.

In conclusion, the 'listening blind spot' is a widespread issue that hinders effective communication and relationship building. However, by practicing active listening and becoming more attuned to non-verbal cues, we can overcome this challenge. It is essential to remember that listening is not merely about hearing words; it is about understanding the complete message being communicated. This understanding forms the foundation of effective communication, fostering empathy, enhancing learning, and strengthening relationships.

Chapter 11
Health, Wealth & Purpose

In our fast-paced modern world, achieving a balance of health, wealth, and purpose has become increasingly important. These three pillars are integral to our overall well-being and success. They are interconnected and often influence one another, creating a delicate balance that requires careful management.

Health, both physical and mental, is the foundation of our existence. It is the vehicle that allows us to navigate through life. Without good health, wealth and purpose would be meaningless. In our modern world, where sedentary lifestyles and processed foods are common, maintaining good health has become a challenge. However, by adopting a balanced diet, regular exercise, and good sleep habits, we can maintain our health. Mental health, too, should not be neglected. Practices like mindfulness, meditation, and maintaining positive relationships can help to keep stress at bay and promote mental well-being.

Wealth, in this context, extends beyond mere financial stability. It encompasses resources such as time, knowledge, and skills. Good healthcare, education, and other resources are necessary for a contented life. In the modern world, achieving wealth often requires hard work, smart planning, and financial literacy. It's essential to invest in oneself through education and skills development, to increase earning potential, whilst simultaneously understanding financial management can be important.

Purpose is the driving force guiding the direction to our lives, in our decision-making and shaping our experiences. Having a clear sense of purpose can make life more meaningful, as it provides motivation, increases resilience, and leads to higher levels of satisfaction. Finding purpose is a personal journey that requires self-reflection. It might be found in a fulfilling career, in service to others, or in the pursuit of a passion. Whatever it is, our purpose should resonate with our values and aspirations.

Balancing health, wealth, and purpose is a dynamic process that requires continuous effort. It starts with self-awareness, understanding our needs, values, and aspirations. Once we know what we want, we can set realistic goals and plan steps to achieve them. It's essential to regularly review these goals and make adjustments as needed.

Maintaining balance requires setting boundaries in our pursuit of wealth, we must not sacrifice our health or lose sight of our purpose. Similarly, our purpose should not drive us to ruin our health or financial stability.

Having a purpose-driven life or business offers numerous benefits and substantially adds value to our existence and endeavours. Here are some reasons why living a purpose-driven life or operating a purpose-driven business is valuable:

Direction and Focus

Purpose provides a clear roadmap for where we want to go, enabling us to focus our efforts effectively. It helps us avoid distractions and stay on the right path.

Motivation and Resilience

When we have a purpose, we're driven to take action, even when faced with adversity. Purpose fuels motivation and fosters resilience, allowing us to overcome challenges and bounce back from setbacks more quickly.

Fulfilment and Satisfaction

Living a purpose-driven life or running a purpose-driven business brings a deep sense of fulfilment. When we know that our actions align with our core values and contribute to something bigger, we experience heightened satisfaction.

Improved Performance

For businesses, having a clear purpose beyond just profit can enhance overall performance. It can attract and retain talent, foster employee engagement, and command customer loyalty. Studies have shown that purpose-driven businesses often outperform their competitors in the long run.

Positive Impact

A purpose-driven life or business often prioritises making a positive impact on society or the environment. This focus on serving others or addressing societal challenges brings about meaningful change and leaves a lasting legacy.

Health and Longevity

Research suggests that having a sense of purpose can enhance our health and even prolong our lives. It can reduce stress, lower the risk of disease, and improve mental health.

Decision Making

Purpose serves as a guiding principle in decision-making processes. It helps to clarify what opportunities to pursue and which ones to let go, both in personal life and business.

A purpose-driven life or business is not just about achieving goals, but also about the journey and the impact made along the way. It infuses our lives and work with meaning, propels us forward with determination and resilience, and allows us to make a significant contribution to the world around us.

Chapter 12
Paying It Forward

'Paying it forward' is a simple yet powerful concept that has the potential to make a significant difference in our world. It refers to the practice of responding to a person's kindness by being kind to someone else, rather than merely repaying the initial favour. It's about creating a chain of goodwill that ripples out into society, touching lives and making a positive impact that goes beyond the immediate recipients.

The concept of paying it forward dates back centuries, with mentions in ancient Greek comedies and religious texts, but it has gained contemporary attention through the 2000 film 'Pay It Forward', where the idea was beautifully illustrated and shared with a wider audience. This principle, when adopted and practiced, can significantly contribute to the enhancement of the social fabric and communal well-being.

The importance of 'paying it forward' can't be overstated. At an individual level, acts of generosity and kindness can brighten someone's day, inspire hope, and alleviate suffering. It can be as simple as a smile, buying a coffee for the person behind you in line, helping a neighbour with their groceries, or volunteering your time for a local charity. These actions may seem small, but they can have a profound effect on the recipient, potentially changing their perspective and encouraging them to extend similar kindness to others.

At a societal level, the ripple effect of 'paying it forward' can foster a more caring and empathetic community. It strengthens social ties and builds trust among individuals, promoting social unity and cohesion. In a world often characterised by division and isolation, these acts of kindness can help bridge gaps and bring people together.

Moreover, 'paying it forward' can also stimulate positive psychological effects. Research has shown that acts of kindness can boost the mood and mental health of both the giver and the receiver. It can instil a sense of purpose and fulfilment, increase happiness, and reduce stress and anxiety. In essence, 'paying it forward' can contribute to overall well-being and happiness in society.

In a business context, 'paying it forward' can enhance corporate social responsibility. Businesses that engage in acts of kindness toward their employees, customers, suppliers or community can foster goodwill, enhance their reputation, and build stronger relationships. This can result in improved employee morale, customer loyalty, and ultimately, business success.

Furthermore, 'paying it forward' can play a crucial role in addressing social issues. For instance, if more people were to contribute their time, skills, or resources to help those less fortunate, it could significantly alleviate problems such as poverty, inequality, and social exclusion.

The concept of 'paying it forward' has deep roots in historical and cultural practices across the globe. Even though the exact phrase 'pay it forward' is relatively new, the underlying principle has been a part of human societies for millennia. One of the earliest recorded instances of the 'pay it forward' concept can be traced back to ancient Greece. In 317 BC, the play 'Dyskolos' by Menander introduced the idea of doing a favour for someone without expecting anything in return, hoping that they would then do the same for others.

The concept also appears in religious teachings. In Christianity, the Bible teaches, "Do to others as you would have them do to you" (Luke 6:31). The Talmud, a central text in Judaism, encourages practitioners to do deeds of loving kindness. In Buddhism, acts of generosity and compassion towards others without expecting anything in return are highly valued.

In 1784, Benjamin Franklin wrote a letter to Benjamin Webb, expressing a variant of the 'pay it forward' concept. He lent Webb some money, not asking for repayment, but instead requesting that Webb assist someone else in need in the future.

The term 'pay it forward' was popularised by Robert A. Heinlein in his book 'Between Planets', published in 1951. Heinlein's character was helped by a stranger, and when he wanted to pay him back, the stranger declined and instead suggested that he find someone else in need and help them.

The concept gained widespread attention and popularity through Catherine Ryan Hyde's 1999 novel 'Pay It Forward', which was later adapted into a movie in 2000. The story revolves around a young boy who, for a school project, develops the 'pay it forward' concept, encouraging good deeds to be repaid by doing good deeds for others rather than the original benefactor.

Since then, 'pay it forward' has become a cultural movement, inspiring numerous acts of kindness and generosity worldwide. Various organisations and initiatives have been established with the sole purpose of promoting and implementing the 'pay it forward' philosophy, demonstrating its timeless relevance and appeal.

The concept of 'paying it forward' is a testament to the power of kindness and generosity. It's a simple philosophy that, if widely adopted, could transform our societies by promoting empathy, unity, and well-being. It can help individuals and societies thrive by creating a culture of kindness where each act of goodwill creates a ripple of positivity. 'Paying it forward' is more than just a concept; it's a lifestyle choice that encourages us to look beyond ourselves and contribute to the greater good. It's a reminder that in a world where we can choose to be anything, choosing to be kind can make all the difference.

If you've not trying 'paying it forward' yet, I can highly recommend it. It will definitely make you feel happier :)

Nature's Gift To Humanity

In nature's embrace, we find our guide,
A teacher wise, standing by our side.
With every whisper of wind and song of bird,
She imparts lessons, too profound to be heard.

She teaches us balance, a delicate dance,
To nourish our souls and give life a chance.
In her gentle rhythm, we learn to be still,
To listen to our hearts and follow our will.

For nature knows the secret to a happy life,
To nurture our mind, body, and soul in strife.
She shows us the way to a contented heart,
To cherish each moment, a precious work of art.

In her vast landscapes, we witness the truth,
That we are all connected, from old to youth.
Like the rivers that flow and the trees that sway,
We need each other to thrive and find our way.

Paying it forward, a lesson she imparts,
To share love and kindness, from our very hearts.
For in giving, we receive blessings untold,
A cycle of abundance, a story to be told.

Nature reminds us of our duty and role,
To care for the Earth, with every heart and soul.
To be stewards of creation, in harmony we strive,

For a sustainable future, where all life can thrive.

So let us learn from nature's wise decree,
To live in harmony, in perfect unity.
With gratitude and love, we'll find our way,
Guided by nature, towards a brighter day.

******

Copyright 2024
All Rights Reserved
Owned by Ian H Bates

******

Notes/Memories/Dreams/Actions
Date:

Notes/Memories/Dreams/Actions
Date:

Notes/Memories/Dreams/Actions
Date:

Notes/Memories/Dreams/Actions
Date:

Notes/Memories/Dreams/Actions
Date:

Notes/Memories/Dreams/Actions
Date:

Notes/Memories/Dreams/Actions
Date:

Notes/Memories/Dreams/Actions
Date:

Notes/Memories/Dreams/Actions
Date:

Notes/Memories/Dreams/Actions
Date:

Notes/Memories/Dreams/Actions
Date:

Notes/Memories/Dreams/Actions
Date:

Notes/Memories/Dreams/Actions
Date:

Notes/Memories/Dreams/Actions
Date:

Notes/Memories/Dreams/Actions
Date:

Notes/Memories/Dreams/Actions
Date:

Notes/Memories/Dreams/Actions
Date:

Notes/Memories/Dreams/Actions
Date:

Notes/Memories/Dreams/Actions
Date:

Notes/Memories/Dreams/Actions
Date:

Notes/Memories/Dreams/Actions
Date:

Notes/Memories/Dreams/Actions
Date:

Notes/Memories/Dreams/Actions
Date:

Notes/Memories/Dreams/Actions
Date:

Notes/Memories/Dreams/Actions
Date:

Notes/Memories/Dreams/Actions
Date:

Notes/Memories/Dreams/Actions
Date:

Notes/Memories/Dreams/Actions
Date:

Notes/Memories/Dreams/Actions
Date:

Notes/Memories/Dreams/Actions
Date:

Notes/Memories/Dreams/Actions
Date:

Notes/Memories/Dreams/Actions
Date:

Notes/Memories/Dreams/Actions
Date:

Notes/Memories/Dreams/Actions
Date:

Notes/Memories/Dreams/Actions
Date:

Notes/Memories/Dreams/Actions
Date:

Notes/Memories/Dreams/Actions
Date:

Notes/Memories/Dreams/Actions
Date:

Notes/Memories/Dreams/Actions
Date:

Notes/Memories/Dreams/Actions
Date:

Notes/Memories/Dreams/Actions
Date:

Notes/Memories/Dreams/Actions
Date:

Notes/Memories/Dreams/Actions
Date:

Notes/Memories/Dreams/Actions
Date:

Notes/Memories/Dreams/Actions
Date:

Notes/Memories/Dreams/Actions
Date:

Notes/Memories/Dreams/Actions
Date:

Notes/Memories/Dreams/Actions
Date:

Notes/Memories/Dreams/Actions
Date:

Notes/Memories/Dreams/Actions
Date:

Notes/Memories/Dreams/Actions
Date:

Notes/Memories/Dreams/Actions
Date:

Notes/Memories/Dreams/Actions
Date:

Notes/Memories/Dreams/Actions
Date:

Notes/Memories/Dreams/Actions
Date:

Notes/Memories/Dreams/Actions
Date:

Notes/Memories/Dreams/Actions
Date:

Notes/Memories/Dreams/Actions
Date:

Notes/Memories/Dreams/Actions
Date:

Notes/Memories/Dreams/Actions
Date:

Notes/Memories/Dreams/Actions
Date:

Notes/Memories/Dreams/Actions
Date:

Notes/Memories/Dreams/Actions
Date:

Notes/Memories/Dreams/Actions
Date:

Notes/Memories/Dreams/Actions
Date:

Notes/Memories/Dreams/Actions
Date:

Notes/Memories/Dreams/Actions
Date:

Notes/Memories/Dreams/Actions
Date:

Notes/Memories/Dreams/Actions
Date:

Notes/Memories/Dreams/Actions
Date:

Notes/Memories/Dreams/Actions
Date:

Notes/Memories/Dreams/Actions
Date:

Notes/Memories/Dreams/Actions
Date:

Notes/Memories/Dreams/Actions
Date:

Notes/Memories/Dreams/Actions
Date:

Notes/Memories/Dreams/Actions
Date:

Notes/Memories/Dreams/Actions
Date:

Notes/Memories/Dreams/Actions
Date:

Notes/Memories/Dreams/Actions
Date:

Notes/Memories/Dreams/Actions
Date:

Notes/Memories/Dreams/Actions
Date:

Notes/Memories/Dreams/Actions
Date:

Notes/Memories/Dreams/Actions
Date:

Printed in Great Britain
by Amazon